MICKEY ROGERS
JOANNE TAYLORE-KNOWLES
STEVE TAYLORE-KNOWLES

SPEAK YOUR MIND

STUDENT'S BOOK
+ access to Student's App and Digital Workbook

2

macmillan education

SCOPE & SEQUENCE

	Outcomes	Vocabulary	Grammar	Speaking
Unit 1 Extraordinary pp. 7–15	• Discuss role models • Talk about a memorable event • Write and talk about an anecdote	• Role models • Reactions • Family situations	• Past progressive • Past progressive vs. simple past Grammar Reference pp. 142–143	• Discuss events in a timeline • Describe personal events • Share anecdotes
	Language and Life—Communication: Present a Citizen Award			
Unit 2 Party! pp. 17–25	• Talk about an idea for a holiday • Talk about money and spending habits • Write about a celebration	• Unique holidays • Money and shopping • Food and drink packaging	• Quantifiers • *enough / not enough* Grammar Reference pp. 143–144	• Talk about new holidays • Discuss opinions about celebrations • Share ideas about special foods
	Language and Life—Creativity: Create a Graduation Ceremony			
Unit 3 What's Trending? pp. 27–35	• Talk about street entertainers in your area • Discuss activities of the past • Write and talk about viewing habits	• Street entertainers • The music industry • TV viewing	• Indefinite pronouns • *used to* Grammar Reference pp. 145–146	• Discuss street entertainers • Compare generations • Talk about TV viewing habits
	Language and Life—Decision-making: Design an Event to Save a Theater			
Unit 4 Your ID pp. 37–45	• Talk about personality types • Describe people with superlatives • Talk about who you are like	• Personality types • Different personalities • Characteristics	• *(not) as … as* • Superlative adjectives Grammar Reference pp. 146–147	• Describe a person's personality • Talk about your personality • Compare family members
	Language and Life—Interpersonal Communication: Understand and Interact with Different Personalities			
Unit 5 Prepping pp. 47–55	• Make predictions and express intentions • Make requests and ask permission • Talk about a social event	• Checking in • Making suggestions • Wedding customs	• Modals of intention, offer, and prediction • Modals of request and permission Grammar Reference pp. 148–149	• Role-play a conversation • Describe plans for a class party • Talk about a social event
	Language and Life—Global Competence: Understand and Appreciate Social Customs			
Unit 6 Changes pp. 57–65	• Talk about risk and change • Discuss life experiences • Discuss positive and negative effects of changes	• Status quo • Life experiences • Changing cities	• Present perfect with *for* and *since* • Present perfect with *ever* and *never* Grammar Reference pp. 149–150	• Discuss changes in your life • Talk about life experiences • Debate changes in your town
	Language and Life—Collaboration: List Recommendations for Visitors Discovering Your Town			

Confident Communicator	Pronunciation	Listening/Reading	Thinking Skills	Writing
Start Talking • Language for speculation *Repair It* • Replacement words *Start Talking* • Sequencing words	• Vowel + consonant + *e*	Read a biography • Skill—Skim a text Listen to people recall memorable events • Skill—Listen for specific information Listen to a story about look-alikes • Skill—Predict the story	• Evaluate • Analyze • Understand	Write an anecdote
Unit Review p. 16 **Study Skills** p. 127—Using Personal Experience				
Keep Talking • Give reasons *Start Talking* • Give opinions *Keep Talking* • Ask follow-up questions	• /tʃ/ and /ʃ/	Read about unofficial celebrations • Skill—Predict the topic Listen to a conversation about the business of holidays • Skill—Identify opinions Listen to a Chinese dumpling recipe • Skill—Listen for specific information	• Analyze • Evaluate	Write about a celebration
Unit Review p. 26 **Follow A Pro** p. 128—A Hotel Manager ▶ An Event Planner				
Start Talking • Make notes *Keep Talking* • Ask for opinions *Keep Talking* • Qualifying phrases	• Reduced form of *used to*	Read a magazine article about street entertainers • Skill—Identify main ideas Listen to an interview with a music producer • Skill—Listen for numbers Listen to a recording about TV viewing habits • Skill—Identify opinions	• Understand • Evaluate	Write about your viewing habits
Unit Review p. 36 **Study Skills** p. 129—Designing a Questionnaire				
Keep Talking • Show disagreement *Keep Talking* • Talk about life events *Keep Talking* • Make comparisons	• Stress on the adjective in *as … as* / *not as … as*	Read an article about personality types • Skill—Summarize Listen to a lecture about personalities of a team • Skill—Identify tone Listen to a recording about family personalities • Skill—Listen for detail	• Apply • Predict	Write about a movie character
Unit Review p. 46 **Follow A Pro** p. 130—A School Psychologist ▶ A Teacher				
Keep Talking • Useful phrases *Keep Talking* • Make requests *Start Talking* • Practice giving a talk	• Word stress with modal auxiliaries	Read a dialogue about a hotel reservation • Skill—Scan Listen to a conversation about a class party • Skill—Listen for gist Listen to a conversation about wedding etiquette • Skill—Listen for main ideas	• Predict • Remember • Analyze	Write about weddings
Unit Review p. 56 **Study Skills** p. 131—Organizing to Help Memorization				
Keep Talking • Useful phrases *Keep Talking* • Reacting to information *Keep Talking* • Point of view	• Present perfect contractions	Read an article about status quo bias • Skill—Identify examples Listen to a recording about bucket lists • Skill—Listen for main ideas Listen to a radio show about changing cities • Skill—Listen for specific information	• Analyze • Create • Understand	Write about your city
Unit Review p. 66 **Follow A Pro** p. 132—An Architect ▶ An Urban Planner				

SCOPE & SEQUENCE

	Outcomes	Vocabulary	Grammar	Speaking
Unit 7 Get to Work pp. 67–75	• Talk about being career-ready • Discuss a successful person • Talk about skills and qualifications	• Career readiness • Success • Employability skills	• Present perfect with *already, yet,* and *just* • Present perfect and simple past Grammar Reference pp. 151–152	• Discuss how career-ready you are • Talk about someone with a nontraditional career • Discuss your creativity
	Language and Life—Problem-solving: Create a Business Plan for an Entrepreneur			
Unit 8 Downtime pp. 77–85	• Talk about kids' activities that adults like doing • Make plans and talk about preferences • Express your opinion	• Kidult activities • Leisure activities • Adjectives of feeling	• Gerund phrases as subject and object • Verb + gerund or infinitive Grammar Reference pp. 152–153	• Explain enjoyable kids' activities • Discuss weekend activities • Talk about doing nothing
	Language and Life—Mindfulness: Select Calming Activities to Relax Your Mind			
Unit 9 Room for Me pp. 87–95	• Talk about types of housing • Talk about living preferences • Discuss future changes in the home	• Housing solutions • Living together • Appliances	• Future forms • Future possibility and certainty Grammar Reference pp. 154–155	• Discuss housing • Talk about future possibilities • Talk about homes of the future
	Language and Life—Decision-making: Use a Decision Matrix to Plan and Develop a Neighborhood			
Unit 10 Wellbeing pp. 97–105	• Talk about study habits • Talk about hypothetical conditions • Write about small life changes	• Brain power • Accidents and illnesses • Collocations with *get*	• Zero and first conditional • Second conditional Grammar Reference pp. 155–156	• Express opinions about study habits • Role-play a conversation about illnesses • Discuss getting in shape and healthy
	Language and Life—Critical Thinking: Create Campaigns to Improve Public Health			
Unit 11 Use and Reuse pp. 107–115	• Talk about what things are made of • Talk about inventions and gifts • Discuss uses of plastic	• Product lifecycles • Clothing materials • Collocations connected to materials	• Simple present passive • Simple past passive Grammar Reference pp. 157–158	• Discuss the lifecycle of a plastic bottle • Talk about a gift you received • Compare how you use plastic
	Language and Life—Innovation: Suggest Upcycling Projects			
Unit 12 I'm a Member pp. 117–125	• Talk about social groups • Discuss networking • Talk about belonging to youth tribes	• Types of community • Networking • Appearance	• Reflexive pronouns • Review of tenses Grammar Reference pp. 158–159	• Discuss social groups • Talk about expanding your network • Discuss subcultures
	Language and Life—Media Literacy: Design an Ad Campaign to Reach a Target Group			

Confident Communicator	Pronunciation	Listening/Reading	Thinking Skills	Writing
Keep Talking • Give negative answers *Keep Talking* • Express doubt *Start Talking* • Describe images	• /j/ and /dʒ/	Read an informative article about career readiness • Skill—Understand vocabulary in context Listen to an interview with an entrepreneur • Skill—Understand attitude Listen to a lecture about employability skills • Skill—Identify key words	• Summarize • Analyze	Write a personal statement
Unit Review p. 76 **Study Skills** p. 133—Creativity				
Start Talking • Describe an activity *Keep Talking* • Agree with a proposal *Start Talking* • Explain a concept	• *–ould* words	Read an article about kidult activities • Skill—Read for main ideas Listen to people plan weekend activities • Skill—Listen for details Listen to a class discussion about the psychology of doing nothing • Skill—Listen for reasons	• Apply • Analyze • Understand	Write a blog entry
Unit Review p. 86 **Follow A Pro** p. 134—A Resort Activities Coordinator A Recreation Coordinator				
Keep Talking • Ask for opinions *Keep Talking* • Ask for reasons for opinions *Keep Talking* • Give reasons for opinions	• /aʊ/ and /oʊ/	Read an article about housing solutions • Skill—Predict Listen to a conversation about where to live • Skill—Listen for attitude Listen to a talk about solar panels • Skill—Take notes	• Understand • Evaluate	Write an opinion paragraph
Unit Review p. 96 **Study Skills** p. 135—Problem Solving				
Start Talking • State agreement or disagreement *Keep Talking* • Ask about an illness *Start Talking* • Make a statement stronger	• Intonation in conditional sentences	Read an article on ways to improve your memory • Skill—Scan Listen to an interview with a health expert • Skill—Listen for cause and effect Listen to a dialogue about a fitness program • Skill—Listen for gist	• Brainstorm • Evaluate • Understand	Write a website comment
Unit Review p. 106 **Follow A Pro** p. 136—A Family Physician A Physical Therapist				
Start Talking • Order steps in a process *Keep Talking* • State who made something *Start Talking* • State alternatives	• Silent *t*	Read an article about the lifecycle of a T-shirt • Skill—Understand words from context Listen to an interview about accidental discoveries • Skill—Listen for key words Listen to a lecture on upcycling items • Skill—Listen for gist	• Brainstorm • Understand • Analyze	Write an email
Unit Review p. 116 **Study Skills** p. 137—Using Precise Language in Academic Writing				
Start Talking • Make a guess *Start Talking* • Show certainty *Keep Talking* • Further a point	• /s/ vs. /ʃ/	Read an article on types of community • Skill—Understand the main ideas Listen to a podcast about networking • Skill—Listen for the main ideas Listen to an interview about different social groups • Skill—Listen for gist	• Analyze • Understand	Write a description
Unit Review p. 126 **Follow A Pro** p. 138—An Entrepreneur An Entrepreneur				

Grammar Quiz: What Do You Already Know?

A Complete the conversation with words from the box.

are is 'm not 's 's what's

Esme: Hi, my name's Esme. **1** ________ your name?
Monique: My name **2** ________ Monique.
Esme: Nice to meet you, Monique. Where **3** ________ you from?
Monique: I **4** ________ from France. I work here. I'm an interpreter.
Esme: Really? That **5** ________ interesting.
Monique: It **6** ________. I love my job! What about you? Are you American?
Esme: No, I'm **7** ________. I'm British.

B Complete the paragraph with the simple present form of the verbs in parentheses.

My sister, Emily, really **1** ________ (love) her phone. She **2** ________ (check) her phone when she **3** ________ (wake) up. I think she **4** ________ (send) about a hundred text messages a day! She **5** ________ (use) about five different social media sites, too. I **6** ________ (have) a smartphone, too, but I can live without it. I **7** ________ (not need) to post pictures of my food every time I have a nice meal! What about you? How much time **8** ________ you ________ (spend) on your phone?

C Choose the correct option.

Leo: What **1 do you have** / **are you having** for lunch today, Jill?
Jill: Today **2 I'm having** / **I have** noodle salad with shrimp and chili sauce.
Leo: It looks delicious! **3 Did you buy** / **Do you bought** it from the café?
Jill: No, **4 I made it** / **I'm making it** at home. It's cheap, and it's healthy, too.
Leo: I think I **5 should** / **could** start to bring food from home. The cafeteria always **6 serves** / **serving** the same things. I **7 want to** / **want** eat a more balanced diet.

D Find one error in each line of the conversation. Write the corrected sentence.

Rob: Is you almost ready, Julie? **1** ________
Julie: Yes! I'm so excited about going to the Amsterdam! **2** ________
Rob: Where do you want to do when we're there? **3** ________
Julie: I want to go sightseeing around a city. **4** ________
Rob: Yeah, I like to do that, too. Can we go by bicycle? **5** ________
Julie: I'd like to, but I can ride a bike! **6** ________

E Complete the email with words from the box.

a a her 's the the X (no article) your

Hi Malu,

Thanks for your email! I'm really excited about **1** ________ school trip to France next summer. **2** ________ hometown looks beautiful. It's great that there is **3** ________ waterfall just three kilometers away. Is there **4** ________ forest, too? I love **5** ________ trees! Can we climb **6** ________ mountain you told me about? I know the weather is sometimes rainy in France, so I've borrowed my friend **7** ________ waterproof jacket and I've also borrowed **8** ________ walking boots.

See you soon!

Reba

Go to the Grammar Review on pages 140–141

UNIT 1 Extraordinary

WHAT DO YOU ALREADY KNOW?

1 **What extraordinary people do you know? Write their names, countries, and careers in the box.**

2 **IN PAIRS** **Share and compare your words. If possible, add more words to the box.**

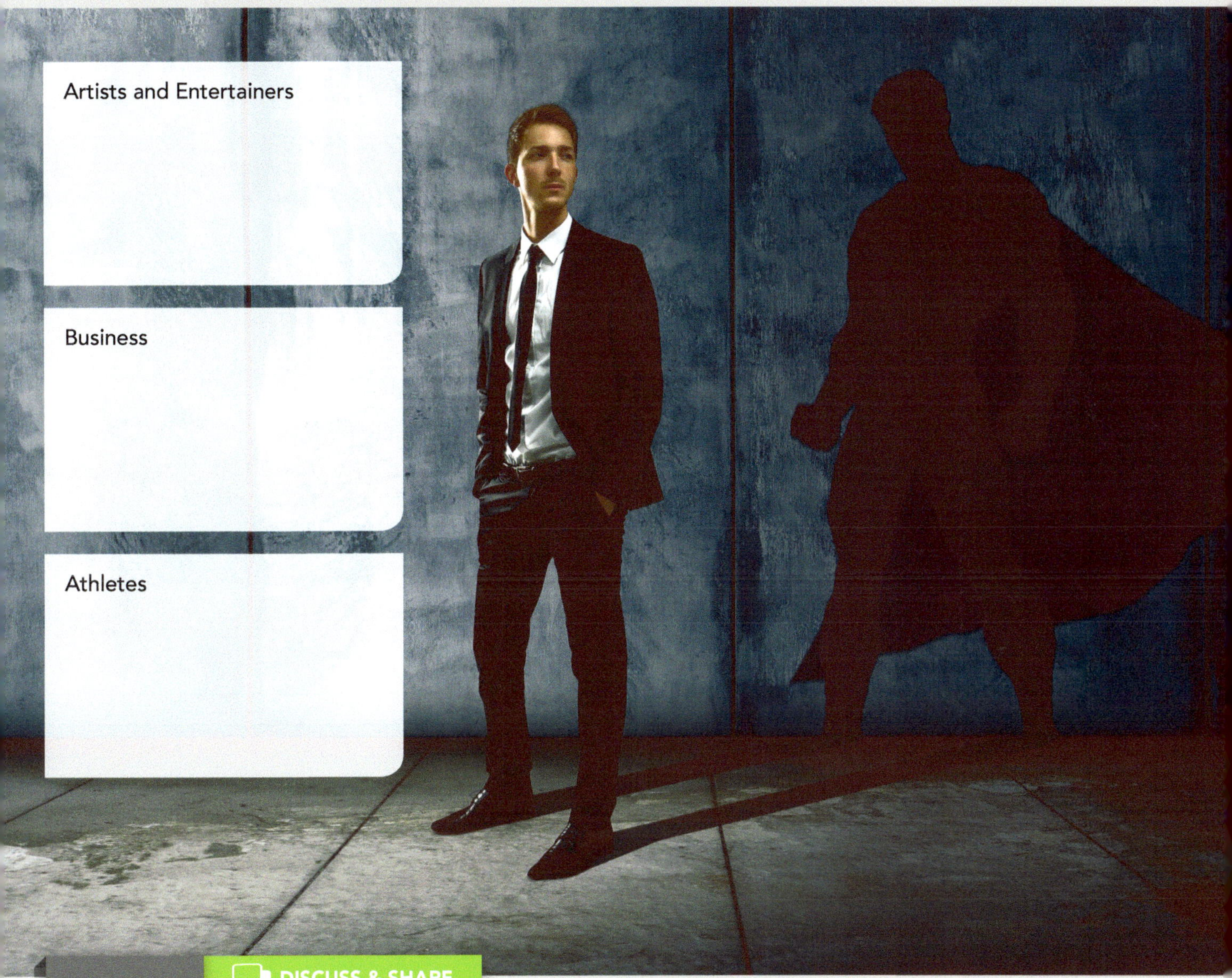

Artists and Entertainers

Business

Athletes

VIDEO

DISCUSS & SHARE

3 **IN GROUPS** **Watch the video and answer the question.**

SYM Is being famous the same as being extraordinary?

In this unit, you will ...

- talk about a role model, describe a memorable event, and tell an anecdote.
- use thinking skills: evaluate, analyze, and understand.
- read a biography.
- use strategies to speculate about reasons, sequence events, use words you know when you don't know an exact word.
- use communication skills to give a short speech for a citizen award.
- learn strategies for using personal experience in writing.

READING

A Do you have any role models? Why do you admire them?

B 1.01 READING SKILL—Skim a text Look at the text quickly for one minute. Don't try to read every word. Then close your book and note down any information you remember.

LILA DOWNS

My role model is Lila Downs. She was born in Oaxaca, Mexico, in 1968. She is a Mexican American singer-songwriter and actress. At the age of eight, she started singing mariachi songs. She became a professional singer when she was at school. Her family **emigrated** from Mexico to the US when she was 14. While they were living there, her father died. After that, Lila and her mother moved back to Mexico.

While she was working in her mother's store, she met her future husband, the musician Paul Cohen. He had a business in the US, so Lila moved from Oaxaca to Minnesota. She went to the University of Minnesota. While she was studying there, she started a music group called La Trova Serrana. It was very **successful**, and Lila decided to leave school to **focus on** music. Lila had a small **role** in the movie *Frida* and worked on the music for the movie *Like Water for Chocolate*. Here are three things you probably don't know about Lila:

- In 2010, while she was traveling the world on her Black Magic Woman Tour, she **revealed** that she had an adopted son named Benito Dxuladi.
- In 2014, scientists named an **insect** after her. The Liladownsia fraile is a very colorful grasshopper. They named it after her because Lila often wears colorful, traditional clothes.
- She sings in Spanish, English, and her native language of Mixtec.

I really **look up to** Lila Downs because she looks for ways to **improve** people's lives through music. I'd love to meet her and ask her this question: "What were you singing about in the song 'Shake Away'?"

C Scan the article in B and answer the questions.

1 Where is Lila from? ____________________

2 How old was Lila when she moved to the US? ____________________

3 When did Lila reveal that she had adopted her son? ____________________

4 What type of animal did scientists name after Lila? ____________________

5 What languages does Lila sing in? ____________________

D Read the article in B in detail to check your answers.

E THINKING SKILL—Evaluate Is it important to have role models? Are most famous people good role models? Discuss and give examples.

VOCABULARY

A Match the bold words from the text in READING B to the definitions.

1 ____________: left your country to move to a different country (verb)

2 ____________: admire; think someone is a good role model (phrasal verb)

3 ____________: make something better (verb)

4 ____________: told a secret (verb)

5 ____________: a small animal with six legs and wings (noun)

6 ____________: achieving wealth, admiration, or popularity (adjective)

7 ____________: pay attention to; concentrate on (phrasal verb)

8 ____________: a part in a movie or a play (noun)

MAKE IT YOURS

Choose a famous role model that you look up to. Find an article about his or her life. Write down any interesting facts that you find in the article.

GRAMMAR past progressive

A Underline the past progressive verb forms in READING B.

While they were living there, her father died.

B Complete the rules with words from the box.

–ing were continued was

1 The past progressive describes actions that began in the past and ____________ for some time.
2 The past progressive always includes the form ____________ or ____________.
3 In the past progressive, add ____________ to the base form of the verb.

For more practice, go to page 142.

C Complete the conversation with the past progressive form of the verb in parentheses.

Ben: I called you last night, but you didn't answer. What **1** ________________ (you do)?
Ashley: We **2** ________________ (celebrate) my great-grandfather's 100th birthday.
Ben: Really? One hundred! That's amazing. Was he your role model while you **3** ________________ (grow) up?
Ashley: Yes, definitely. He was my hero! He **4** ________________ (open) presents when you called. Everyone **5** ________________ (clap).
Ben: I'm sure he had a great time yesterday.
Ashley: I think so. We **6** ________________ (not plan) for the party to end at midnight!

D IN PAIRS Ask and answer the questions.

1 What were you doing …
a in the summer? **b** in 2016? **c** last Thursday? **d** last night?

A: What were you doing last night? *B: I was visiting my grandparents.*

SPEAKING

A Read about Ann Makosinski, a young inventor and role model. Why is she famous?

Ann Makosinski
1997—born October 3, Canada
2011—in Philippines, her friend fails exam because there's no electricity at night
2011—Ann gets idea for flashlight
2012—develops flashlight powered by body heat

B IN PAIRS Discuss the events in Ann's life using information from the notes.

C IN GROUPS Discuss how you think Ann's flashlight works. Use the Confident Communicator box to help you.

CONFIDENT COMMUNICATOR
START TALKING

Use the following expressions to talk about something you are not 100% sure about:
I'm not sure, but I think it may/could be …
Maybe it works without …
Perhaps/Maybe you can use it …

VOCABULARY reactions

A Match the sentences (1–6) to the pictures (a–f). Write the letter.

a

b

c

d

e

f

1 Were you **disappointed** that you didn't get a good grade? _____
2 Walt's phone rang in the middle of the night. He was **worried**. _____
3 There was a snake crossing the path. I was so **scared**. I'm afraid of snakes! _____
4 I won a free trip around the world. I'm **thrilled**! _____
5 I was **glad** the bus came. It was raining very heavily. _____
6 I'm **confused**! Which way do I go? _____

LISTENING

A 1.02 LISTENING SKILL—Listen for specific information **Listen to four people talk about memorable events. Match the speakers (1–4) to how they felt (a–d).**

1 Katrin: _____ a thrilled
2 Giovanni: _____ b glad
3 Kyle: _____ c worried
4 Gemma: _____ d confused

B THINKING SKILL—Analyze **Why do you think the speakers felt the way they did? Evaluate if you would feel the same way.**

I think Katrin was worried because she loves animals. I would feel …

PRONUNCIATION vowel + consonant + *e*

A 1.03 **Listen and notice the change in the vowel sounds. The *e* changes the vowel to a long sound.**

Suddenly, a police officer shouted, "**Hide**!"
We **hid** in a café.

B 1.04 **Practice saying the words. Listen and check your pronunciation.**

1 hid hide 2 at ate 3 mad made 4 rid ride

GRAMMAR past progressive vs. simple past

A Underline the action in progress and circle the action that interrupts it.

1 I was watching the game at my friend's house when the phone rang.
2 I was working for NASA on the Mars mission when it happened.
3 My boss called me in the middle of the night while I was sleeping.
4 When the plane came down, we were staying in a hotel.

B Choose the correct option to complete the grammar rules.

1 The past progressive describes an **interrupting action** / **action in progress**.
2 The simple past describes the **interrupting action** / **action in progress**.
3 We use ***when*** / ***while*** to introduce the action in progress.
4 We use ***when*** / ***while*** to introduce the interrupting action.
5 We use a comma after *when* and *while* clauses at the **beginning** / **end** of a sentence.

For more practice, go to page 142.

C Complete the text with the correct form of the verb in parentheses. Use the past progressive or the past simple.

Kiera: Did you hear that news story about the animal rescue?
Asha: No. What **1** ________________ (happen)?
Kiera: I **2** ________________ (read) about it on the way to work yesterday. Well, you know there was that hurricane in Texas? Hurricane Harvey, I think it was.
Asha: Yes, I remember it.
Kiera: Well, after the hurricane, when people **3** ________________ (leave) their homes, there were lots of pets that **4** ________________ (live) on the streets. The animal rescue centers had no room for them. So, an airline organized a flight to take about 60 of the animals from Houston to San Diego to find new forever homes! I **5** ________________ (cry) when I read the story. There was a photo of the pilot and he **6** ________________ (hold) some of the puppies. They were so cute!
Asha: The perfect happy ending, huh?

D IN PAIRS What happened on your way to class today? Describe the actions in progress and interrupting actions.

A: While I was walking to class today, I saw my friend Gabriel.

B: My phone rang while I was getting on the bus.

SPEAKING

A Think about a memorable event in your life. Make notes about:

- what happened
- where you were
- when it happened
- what you were doing
- how you felt

B IN GROUPS Take turns describing the events. Ask questions about the details. Use the Confident Communicator box to help you.

A: I remember the storm in 2016. I was living in Monterrey at the time. It started raining while I was walking to work.

B: Were you scared?

CONFIDENT COMMUNICATOR
REPAIR IT

If you don't know a word in English, here are some things you can do:
Use a word that means something similar (e.g., *very worried* for *scared*).
Give a short description of the event (e.g., *a lot of rain* for *storm*).

LESSON 3 Coincidences

VOCABULARY family situations

A Match the words and phrases from the box to the pictures (1–8).

adopted divorced engaged large family only child single single parent twins

1 
______

2 
______

3 
______

4 
______

5 
______

6 
______

7 
______

8 
______

B Complete the sentences with the words and phrases from A.

1 My sister and I are ______. She was born 10 minutes before I was. We look the same, but we are different.
2 Jack comes from a ______. He has eight brothers and sisters.
3 I am ______, but I want to get married in the future.
4 I am an ______. When I was growing up, I wanted a brother or sister.
5 My parents are ______. My mom got married again last year.
6 Dan is a/an ______. His wife died about five years ago, so he takes care of his kids on his own.
7 We got ______ last year. We're getting married this summer.
8 Lois's parents ______ her when she was six weeks old.

C IN PAIRS Discuss your family. Ask questions to find out more information.

LISTENING

A Look at the picture. What do you notice about the people?

B 1.05 LISTENING SKILL—Predict the story
Listen to the first half of an anecdote about an amazing coincidence. What do you think will happen next?

C 1.06 Listen to the second half of the anecdote to check. Were you correct?

D 1.07 **Now listen to the whole anecdote. Circle the sequencing phrases you hear.**

about two years ago
about six months ago
a week later
a month later
about a month after that
about three months later
later that day
later on
the next day
a few days later
finally
in the end

E THINKING SKILL—Understand **What was the coincidence in this anecdote? Summarize.**

MAKE IT REAL

To show you are surprised about something in an anecdote or story, you can say:
You're kidding! *That's unbelievable!* *No way!*

WRITING

A Read this anecdote about an amazing coincidence. What do you think is interesting about it?

This is an anecdote a friend told me. It's about a woman who was adopted at six months old. One day, she was in the hair salon in the new neighborhood she was living in, when she saw a woman who looked similar to her. They talked a little bit about their lives. The young woman said she was adopted as a baby.

"When's your birthday?" asked the older woman.

"January 25, 1998," said the young woman. The older woman was shocked.

"I gave a daughter up for adoption. She was born on January 25, 1998," she said.

After that, they both took a DNA test and discovered they were mother and daughter. They were so glad to find one another. I think this story is interesting because it is an amazing coincidence.

B Think of an interesting anecdote that happened to you or someone you know. Make notes about the following:

- who the anecdote involves
- what happened
- where it happened
- what the people were doing
- how they felt
- why you think the anecdote is interesting

C Write the main events of your anecdote.

____

____

____

D Write your anecdote in your notebook. Make sure that the events are in the correct order.

E IN PAIRS **Share your writing. What was interesting about your partner's anecdote?**

SPEAKING

A Think of an interesting anecdote you read in a book, heard on the news, or saw on TV.

B IN GROUPS **Share your anecdotes. Decide on the anecdote that you all like. Use the Confident Communicator box to help you.**

CONFIDENT COMMUNICATOR
START TALKING

Use sequencing words and phrases to connect the events in an anecdote.
About three months ago … / Two weeks ago … / Last week …
After that … / Then …
In the end … / Finally …

Language and Life

Communication – Citizen Award

A What is a hero? Do you know of any heroes in your community?

B 1.08 Read the magazine article about heroes. Then choose *True* or *False*.

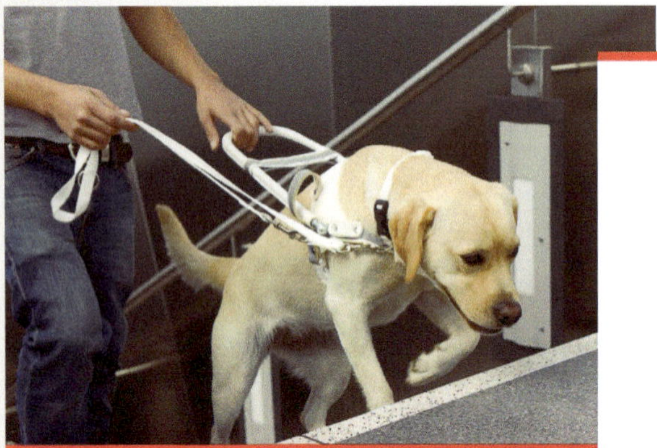

Victor Karlsson

Meet 20-year-old Victor Karlsson from Malmo, Sweden. When Victor was eight years old, he became blind in an accident. With help from his family and friends, Victor is now a local hero in Malmo. Victor and his guide dog Charlie are helping improve the lives of blind children and adults by raising money. In 2018, Victor raised 1,500 euros walking 111 km between Malmo and Copenhagen. In 2020, he is planning to run a half-marathon. "Everyone looks up to Victor," says his friend Katya. "He's a true role model."

Petra Gonzalez

Nineteen-year-old Petra Gonzalez saved her sister from a fire in their home in Mexico. Petra, a university student, woke up one night to the smell of smoke. She woke up her sister. She was carrying her sister out of their apartment when she saw the fire on the other side of the house. Amazingly, firefighters arrived in time to save both girls. Petra got an award from the local mayor. "I was really scared," said Petra, "but I was just doing what any sister would do."

Mimi Kallas

While Mimi Kallas was working in a tourist office in her home town in Greece, she noticed men and women on the streets asking for food. Mimi stopped working at her job and started a food service for homeless people. She collects extra food from stores and cooks up to 100 meals a day in the kitchen of a school. She gives out the food for free to anyone who needs it. "Without Mimi, we couldn't survive," said one man. "She is an amazing woman. I'm so glad she is here to help us."

1 Victor was eight when he went blind. True / False
2 Victor ran a half-marathon in 2018. True / False
3 Petra is an only child. True / False
4 The fire was in Petra's school. True / False
5 Mimi works in a tourist office. True / False
6 Mimi cooks food for people at a school. True / False

C IN PAIRS Discuss why each person from B is a hero. Give reasons.

A: Who do you think is the most heroic?

B: I think … is the most heroic because …

A: Oh, really? I think … is the most heroic because …

D IN GROUPS Imagine you work for a local community committee. You want to offer a Citizen Award to a person who did something extraordinary. Research news websites online to find examples of heroic acts and write a list.

This woman in Sao Paulo is a hero. She saved a child's life.

______

______

______

______

E IN GROUPS Role-play an awards ceremony where the heroes are given their awards and make short thank-you speeches.

A: Please welcome …, who gets a Citizen Award today for helping out every week at the local baseball club …

B: I'd like to say how thrilled I am to get this award. I love helping out at the local baseball club because …

F Discuss the questions.

1 Did you clearly communicate the reasons for giving the award? Why or why not?
2 In what other situations does a group of people decide who wins an award?

MAKE IT DIGITAL

Go online and find examples of heroic acts in your country. Talk about which ones you think are extraordinary and why.

VOCABULARY review

SCORE: / 10

A Choose the correct option.

1 Raul was **glad** / **disappointed** when he got bad grades in his final exams.
2 Were you **scared** / **thrilled** when you heard a hurricane was coming?
3 Please don't talk to me while I'm studying, or I will get **glad** / **confused**.
4 I'm a little **worried** / **disappointed** about tomorrow's party. What will happen if people don't come?
5 My parents were **scared** / **thrilled** when I told them I got an award.
6 Jackson **is** / **isn't** an only child. He has a brother named Harrison.
7 Dad comes from a **large** / **small** family. He has five brothers and two sisters.
8 Pavlos and Christina got **adopted** / **divorced**. Pavlos is getting married again next month.
9 My parents got **engaged** / **adopted** when they were in their 30s.
10 I'm **an only parent** / **a single parent**, but the kids see their dad on the weekends.

GRAMMAR review

SCORE: / 10

A Correct the errors and rewrite the sentences.

1 What you were doing last New Year's Eve? ____________________
2 In 2016, I living in Mexico City. ____________________
3 At noon, my friends and I were eat lunch. ____________________
4 My brother were making breakfast this morning. ____________________
5 They was watching a movie last night. ____________________

B Unscramble and write.

1 started raining / While / was / for the bus, / it / waiting / I ____________________
2 while / The movie / our tickets / started / we / buying / were ____________________
3 rang / was / I / my phone / working / when ____________________
4 swimming / We / were / when / happened / the accident ____________________
5 got / watching TV / The kids / when / home / were / their father ____________________

16–20 correct: You can discuss family situations and reactions. You can use the past progressive.
0–15 correct: Look again at the Vocabulary and Grammar sections in the unit.

TOTAL SCORE: / 20

WHAT DO YOU KNOW NOW? Look back at page 7 and add words you know now to the boxes.

STUDY SKILLS USING PERSONAL EXPERIENCE

Take the quiz. Then go to Study Skills on page 127.
Find the answers and learn more about using personal experience.

1 Which two of the following things do we usually find in personal narratives?
a evidence **b** feelings **c** descriptions

2 Personal narratives are usually subjective.
a True **b** False

3 Which two of the following things do we usually find in factual accounts?
a chronological events **b** numbers and statistics **c** use of the word *I*

UNIT 2

Party!

WHAT DO YOU ALREADY KNOW?

1 Think about occasions you celebrate. Write the words.

2 IN PAIRS Share and compare your ideas. Think of more words to add to each category.

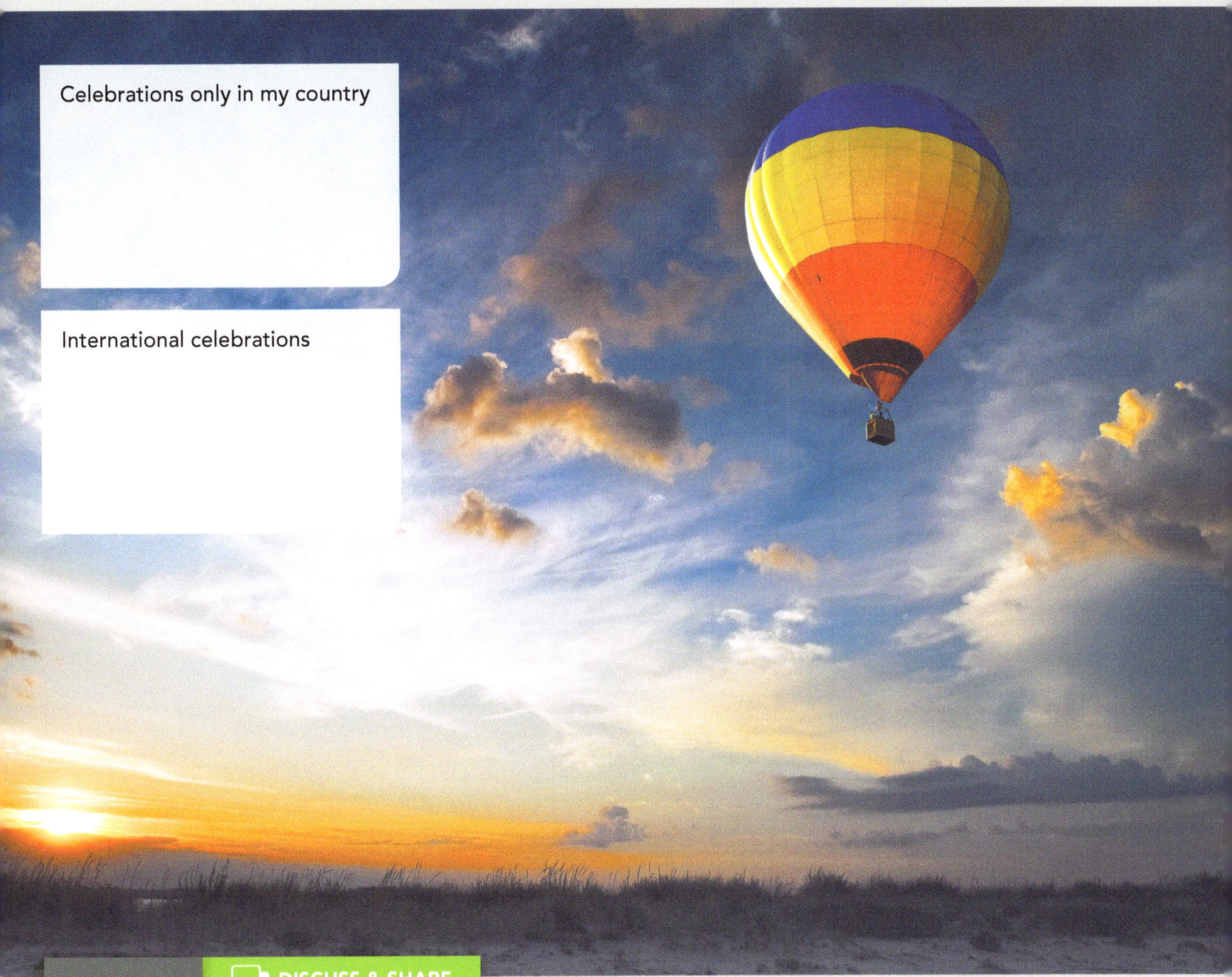

Celebrations only in my country

International celebrations

VIDEO

DISCUSS & SHARE

3 IN GROUPS Watch the video and answer the question.

SYM Do you prefer to buy gifts or buy experiences for celebrations?

In this unit, you will ...

- talk about official and unofficial holidays, spending habits, and celebrations.
- use thinking skills: analyze and evaluate.
- read about unusual holidays.
- use strategies to start and keep talking by giving reasons, giving opinions, and asking follow-up questions.
- use creativity skills to work with others and create your own graduation ceremony.
- follow a hotel manager to learn about the jobs and skills needed in the hospitality industry.

Days of the Year

READING

A Look at the pictures in B. What are the people doing?

B READING SKILL—Predict the topic Read the title and look at the pictures. What do you think you are going to read about? Check (✓) one of the ideas.

- ☐ a story about someone's birthday
- ☐ an article about celebrating unusual days of the year
- ☐ a blog about celebrations around the world

EVERY DAY *is a* HOLIDAY!

Take a look at your **calendar** for the year ahead. Some dates show an **official** event that people **celebrate** somewhere in the world. For example, Americans celebrate Independence Day on July 4. On October 8, the Japanese celebrate Health and Sports Day. A lot of people **get the day off** work, and schools and businesses are closed. People may eat special food on these days or give and **receive** gifts.

Then, there are unofficial holidays. These are days when people sometimes **arrange** a party at school or at work. Unofficial holidays celebrate unimportant and fun things like food, movies, books, and TV shows.

To show you what I mean, last week, a **colleague** said, "It's 'Take a Selfie Day'! Today you can take a lot of selfies." In my opinion, there's too much time spent taking selfies—you don't need a special day for it!

There are a few websites that list all these celebrations. Think of any day of the year, and there is something to celebrate. I learned there are days of the year for everything: Read in the Bathtub Day (February 9), World Yoga Day (February 22), and my favorite, Make Music Day (June 21). A lot of days celebrate food, like Caesar Salad Day on July 4 and Eat a Peach Day on August 22. There are too many dates for me to remember!

I am thinking of asking my **boss** if I can get the day off on the second Friday of March. It's World Sleep Day. And a little advice for you—don't think of asking me to do anything on Lazy Day (August 10)!

C 2.01 Read the text in B to check your answer.

D Read the text again and choose the correct option.

		a	b
1	When do people in Japan celebrate Health and Sports Day?	**a** July 4	**b** October 8
2	Who told the writer about Take a Selfie Day?	**a** her boss	**b** a colleague
3	What is the writer's favorite Day of the Year?	**a** Make Music Day	**b** World Yoga Day
4	What day of the week is World Sleep Day on?	**a** Monday	**b** Friday

E THINKING SKILL—Analyze What holidays are celebrated in your country but not in other countries?

VOCABULARY

A Match the bold words from the text in READING B to the definitions.

1. agreed upon or arranged by people in power (adjective) ____________
2. a chart with days of the year showing seasonal information (noun) ____________
3. when you don't have to go to work or school (phrase) ____________
4. do something to recognize an important or special event (verb) ____________
5. a person who is in charge at work (noun) ____________
6. make plans for an event (verb) ____________
7. get something from someone (verb) ____________
8. a person you work with (noun) ____________

MAKE IT YOURS

Search online for "days of the year" and find more fun holidays. Select a day and share it with your classmates.

GRAMMAR quantifiers

A **Look back at the text in READING B. Circle these words: *some, a lot of, a little, too many, any, too much, a few.* Underline the noun that follows. Write the phrases in the correct column.**

Countable	Uncountable
some dates	

B **Choose the correct option to complete the grammar rules.**

1. Use *some* with countable nouns / uncountable nouns / both.
2. Use *a lot of* with countable nouns / uncountable nouns / both.
3. Use *a little* with countable nouns / uncountable nouns / both.
4. Use *too many* with countable nouns / uncountable nouns / both.
5. Use *any* with countable nouns / uncountable nouns / both.
6. Use *too much* with countable nouns / uncountable nouns / both.
7. Use *a few* with countable nouns / uncountable nouns / both.

For more practice, go to page 143.

C **Choose the correct quantifier.**

Pasteles de hoja are a popular dish in Puerto Rico, but they are also made in the Dominican Republic, Colombia, and El Salvador. They are usually made around Christmas and families often spend **1 a little / a few** days preparing them. It's common to make **2 a lot of / a few** pasteles at the same time (usually between 50 and 200!). Here is the basic recipe: Make a vegetable dough from green banana flour. Fill the dough with **3 some / a few** meat. Don't add **4 too many / too much** meat because you have to add the chickpeas, raisins, and olives, too. Wrap the pasteles in banana leaves and steam them. People usually freeze some of them to enjoy on Three Kings Day on January 6. Or they take **5 a little / some** boxes of pasteles as a gift to family or friends. They are delicious, but very big, so you may not want to eat **6 too much / too many**!

D IN PAIRS **Think about a celebration that you went to recently that had food and drinks. What did you have? Discuss. Use quantifiers where necessary.**

I went to a party for my colleague's birthday. There was a lot of food. I had a few sandwiches and some salad.

SPEAKING

A **March 26 is Make Up Your Own Holiday Day. On this day you can choose to celebrate anything you like. Think about what you would like to celebrate on this holiday. Make notes about:**

- the name of your holiday
- what you do to celebrate it
- where you want to celebrate
- why you want to celebrate it

B IN GROUPS **Share your ideas about your own holiday. Use the Confident Communicator box to help you. Whose ideas do you like best? Why?**

CONFIDENT COMMUNICATOR
KEEP TALKING

Use *because* and *because of* to give reasons.
Because + subject + verb
I'd like to make a holiday for pets because *I think …*
Because of + noun
I probably won't celebrate the day at the beach because of *the weather. It's too hot.*

The Business of Holidays

VOCABULARY money and shopping

A Match the underlined phrases (1–6) to the definitions (a–f). Write the letter.

1 I love traveling, so I usually spend money on trips abroad. ____
2 You can make money by selling handmade gifts online. ____
3 I don't like to lend money to friends. ____
4 I never waste money on things I don't need. ____
5 It's easy to overspend at certain times of the year. I spend too much money at Thanksgiving. ____
6 Sometimes I borrow money from my parents, but I always pay it back. ____

a get money by working or selling something
b ask someone to give you money because you don't have enough
c buy things you don't need
d buy something
e give someone money because they don't have enough
f spend more money than you have

MAKE IT REAL

There are many informal synonyms for money in English. Here are a few: *cash, bucks, loot, bread, dough, capital.*

B Choose the correct option to complete the text.

Are you looking for extra ways to **1** make / spend money? Instead of **2** borrowing / lending money from a friend or member of your family, here are a few simple ideas to help:

- Don't **3** waste / lend money on expensive gifts when, with a little imagination, you can make your own. How about making cookies and giving them as gifts to family and friends?
- Many stores have sales in January. It's easy to find things at good prices at this time of year. Buy the items you need to make your card and gifts. Decide how much you can afford so you don't **4** waste / overspend.

C IN PAIRS Ask and answer questions using the phrases in A.

A: Do you lend money to friends? *B: Sometimes, if they really need it.*

LISTENING

A 2.02 LISTENING SKILL—Identify opinions Listen to a conversation in a store. Do you think the man and woman agree or disagree with one another?

B Write the phrases under the correct headings.

Exactly. I know. That's true. You're right.
I disagree. I'm not sure about that. Yeah!

Phrases for agreeing

____ ____
____ ____
____

Phrases for disagreeing

____ ____

C THINKING SKILL—Evaluate Do you agree or disagree that you should never borrow or lend money? Why or why not?

GRAMMAR enough / not enough

A Decide if the nouns that follow *enough* and *not enough* are *Countable* or *Uncountable*.

1 Not enough people shop around these days. ____________

2 They don't have enough money. ____________

3 I have enough decorations. ____________

B Choose the correct option to complete the rules.

1 *Enough* shows that the amount is the right amount / not the right amount.

2 *Not enough* shows that the amount is the right amount / not the right amount.

3 *Enough* and *not enough* are used with countable nouns / uncountable nouns / both.

For more practice, go to page 144.

C Look at the pictures and write sentences with *enough* or *not enough*.

1

2

3

4

1 I / have enough / money / buy / this hat.

____

2 There / be enough / eggs / make / the cake.

____

3 She / have enough / food / on her plate.

____

4 He / have enough / casual / shoes.

____

D IN PAIRS Do you think there are enough national celebrations throughout the year in your country? Discuss the days in the year when people get the day off.

SPEAKING

A Do you think some people spend a lot of money on celebrations these days? On which celebrations?

B IN PAIRS Discuss your opinions about what people spend money on for different celebrations. Use the Confident Communicator box to help you.

CONFIDENT COMMUNICATOR
START TALKING

Use informal or formal language depending on your situation.

Informal
I think people waste money on decorations for holidays.
I don't think it's a good idea to borrow money for celebrations.
I bet some people spend lots of money on gifts.
I guess lending money to a friend is OK.

More formal
In my opinion, people shouldn't feel they have to buy gifts.
From my point of view, Independence Day is an important celebration.

Celebration Food and Drink

VOCABULARY food and drink packaging

A Label the food items in the pictures (1–8) with words from the box.

bag of oranges	box of chocolates	carton of juice	jug of apple cider
bottle of water	can of nuts	jar of olives	package of cookies

1 

______

2 

______

3 

______

4 

______

5 

______

6 

______

7 

______

8 

______

B IN PAIRS What do you usually give or receive as a gift on holidays? Discuss.

A: I usually make cookies and give a box to my friends at Christmas.

B: I get a jar of honey from my aunt. She keeps bees.

LISTENING

A 2.03 You are going to listen to a chef describing food he is making for a special celebration. Listen to the introduction and choose the celebration he is talking about.

1 St. Patrick's Day 2 Thanksgiving 3 Chinese New Year 4 International Women's Day

B 2.04 LISTENING SKILL—Listen for specific information Listen to the recipe and complete each ingredient with one word.

Dumplings (makes about 30)

2 ______ of dumpling wrappers

1 can of water chestnuts

1 ______ of green onions

2 boxes of mushrooms

2 teaspoons of Chinese spices

garlic

small ______ of oil

For the dipping sauce:

1 ______ of sweet chili sauce

ginger

sesame seeds

1/2 ______ of soy sauce

C IN PAIRS **Think about a celebration food that you like. Make a note of the ingredients you need and discuss.**

A: I really love pavlova.
B: What do you need to make it?
A: You need a carton of eggs, a carton of cream, and …

D THINKING SKILL—Evaluate **Which celebration food or drink from your country would you recommend to a foreign visitor? Why?**

PRONUNCIATION /tʃ/ and /ʃ/

A 2.05 **Listen. Notice the difference between the /tʃ/ sound and the /ʃ/ sound.**

1 shop chop **2** ships chips **3** sheep cheap

B 2.05 **Listen again and repeat. Exaggerate the /tʃ/ *and* /ʃ/ sounds as you say the words.**

C IN PAIRS **Practice saying the pairs of words. Can your partner hear the difference between the /tʃ/ *and* /ʃ/ sounds when you say the words?**

WRITING

A **Read the paragraph describing a celebration. What does the festival celebrate? Do you have a celebration like this in your country?**

We celebrate Grand Kadooment Day at the end of the Crop Over festival. A lot of people in the Caribbean celebrate it, too, **but** it's the national celebration of Barbados. In the past, Crop Over was a celebration to mark the end of the sugar cane season. People dress up in costumes or in their best clothes, **and** there are street parades and street food festivals all over the island. We normally eat fried fish **or** fish cakes and sno-cones—ice with flavors such as ginger or coconut. I really like it **because** it's a holiday. We get the day off work, **so** we can have some family time.

B **Match the bold linking words in A to their use.**

1 ____________: introduces a contrasting idea
2 ____________: adds extra information
3 ____________: gives a reason
4 ____________: gives a result
5 ____________: gives an alternative

C **In your notebook, write a short paragraph about a celebration you like. Use linking words to connect your sentences.**

SPEAKING

A **Imagine you are ordering a food gift box online for a friend who lives abroad. You want to add some special celebration foods that are typical of your country. Make a list of the items you would include.**

B IN PAIRS **Show your list to your partner. Add any items from your partner's list that you would like to include. Use the Confident Communicator box to help you.**

C IN GROUPS **Share your ideas with the members of your group. Decide whose gift box you would most like to receive. Explain why.**

CONFIDENT COMMUNICATOR
KEEP TALKING

You can use *Did you* to ask follow-up questions in a conversation. For example:
Did you include a jar of …?
No! I forgot. But I should. I included a box of … Did you?
Yes, I did. You can't celebrate … without those!

Language and Life

Creativity – Graduation Celebrations

A 2.06 **Read an article about different graduation celebrations from around the world. Then choose *Yes* or *No*.**

Graduation Ceremonies
Around the **World**

Sweden

Swedish graduates wear sailor's caps to their graduation ceremony. The ceremony usually starts with singing. Parents arrive and give their children gifts tied with ribbons, and the graduates wear the ribbons around their necks. At the end of the ceremony, there is a parade through the streets of the town, and local people come to congratulate the students.

Japan

In Japan, graduation happens in March, before the new school year. High school students wear their school uniforms for their graduation ceremony. If their school doesn't have a uniform, they wear formal clothes, such as a suit for men and a kimono for women. The principal usually gives a speech. Then, the student president gives a speech.

United States

In the US, it's common for a famous person (sometimes a graduate of the university) or a politician to give a speech to congratulate the graduates. In some large American universities, the ceremony happens in a sports stadium. Students normally wear special caps and gowns in the colors of their university or department.

South Africa

Graduates from the University of Witwatersrand in Johannesburg have an interesting musical tradition. The graduation ceremony there starts with a formal procession by the teachers and workers at the university. After that, they play the song "I Got You (I Feel Good)" by James Brown for the students to dance to.

Argentina

Students in Argentina usually wear old clothes for their graduation ceremony. The reason? Family and friends throw sticky or messy food at the graduates, like flour, eggs, ketchup, and soda. It's supposed to bring them good luck!

1 Graduates in Sweden wear traditional caps and gowns. Yes / No
2 Graduation ceremonies in Japan happen at the end of the year. Yes / No
3 In Argentina, graduates wear formal clothes. Yes / No
4 One university in South Africa plays a particular song at graduation. Yes / No
5 In the US, graduation ceremonies often happen in large outdoor spaces. Yes / No

B **Which graduation ceremony described in A would you like to go to? Why?**

C **IN PAIRS Discuss some of the things that people do in your country to celebrate high school or university graduation. Use the prompts to help you.**

- have a family meal
- celebrate with a night out with friends
- go on vacation with classmates
- have a party at home
- go to a formal organized event
- other: ______________________________

A: People usually celebrate by going to a formal organized event at a hotel or club.

B: Yes, they do. But sometimes they go on vacation with their classmates. We went to …

D **IN GROUPS Imagine you are on the Student Committee at your university. Read the email from the university president and brainstorm ideas for your ideal graduation ceremony.**

New Message

From: johnwilson@university.uni

To: studentcommittee@university.uni   Cc Bcc

Subject: RE: Graduation Speakers

Dear Student Committee members,

As you may know, we are looking for speakers for next year's graduation ceremony. We would like your help in choosing one or two public figures who our graduating students respect and admire. We would also like your thoughts on the following things for the ceremony:

- what students should wear
- where the ceremony should take place
- which students should give a speech
- what music you think should be played

We look forward to your ideas.

Please present your ideas to me at our next meeting on March 15.

Regards,

John Wilson
University President

Send

E **Make a list of one or two suggestions for each of the points in the university president's email.**

____

____

____

____

F **Give a presentation to the class and the university president (your teacher). Which ideas for a graduation ceremony do most people like? Take a vote.**

G **Discuss the questions.**

1 Was it easy or hard to work together to think of creative ideas?
2 In what other situations do you listen to different people offer creative ideas?

MAKE IT DIGITAL

Go online and watch videos of graduation ceremonies from around the world. Which ones do you think you would like to go to?

VOCABULARY review

SCORE: / 10

A Complete the sentences with the words from the box.

bag | boxes | can | jar | package

1 How many ______________ of breakfast cereal do you buy a month?
2 I ate nearly a whole ______________ of chocolate cookies!
3 Dad bought my mom a ______________ of marmalade when he went to Spain.
4 I'd rather get a ______________ of potato chips than a box of raisins for my snack.
5 Do you want to get a ______________ of tomato soup or a bag of tomatoes?

B Choose the best option.

It's easy to **1 overspend / waste** at holidays. I try to **2 borrow / save** some money every week so that I can buy little gifts for everyone in my family. My dad loves chocolate, so I often get him a **3 box / can** of Swiss chocolates. My mom loves scarves, so I shop **4 around / about** to find her pretty ones. My sister's easy to buy for. I usually get her a **5 jug / bottle** of perfume. And then, there's the dog. He always gets a toy!

GRAMMAR review

SCORE: / 10

A Choose the correct option.

1 **A few / lot of** people came to the office party. There were only about 20 people there.
2 This coffee has too **much / many** sugar in it. I can't drink it.
3 **Some / A little** people go to their graduation ceremony in formal clothes!
4 I don't think there are **a little / enough** public holidays in my country.
5 The party dress was too **much / many** money for me to buy.

B Complete the text with the words and phrases from the box.

a few | a lot | enough | some | too many

One country with **1** ______________ of public holidays is Argentina. In total, there are 19 public holidays. **2** ______________ people say that 19 holidays is **3** ______________. Others say that holidays help people relax and that, in general, people don't have **4** ______________ time off work. **5** ______________ countries have a similar number; Colombia has 18 days and Thailand has 16 days.

16–20 correct: You can discuss money, shopping, and food and drink packaging. You can use quantifiers to talk about *enough / not enough*.
0–15 correct: Look again at the Vocabulary and Grammar sections in the unit.

TOTAL SCORE: / 20

WHAT DO YOU KNOW NOW? Look back at page 17 and add the words you know now to the boxes.

FOLLOW A PRO HOSPITALITY

Take the quiz about hospitality. Then go to Follow A Pro on page 128. Find the answers and learn more about the hospitality industry.

1 When did the world's oldest hotel, located in Japan, open?
a 705 **b** 1205 **c** 1505

2 What country gets the most international tourists per year?
a the US **b** China **c** France

3 How many hotel rooms are there in the world (in millions)?
a 5.1 **b** 8.5 **c** 17.2

UNIT 3 What's Trending?

WHAT DO YOU ALREADY KNOW?

1 **Think of TV shows, movies, and music you like. Make a list.**

2 **IN PAIRS** **Share and compare your favorites. Add more things to your lists.**

TV shows

Movies

Music

VIDEO

DISCUSS & SHARE

3 **IN GROUPS** **Watch the video and answer the question.**

Do you prefer to watch entertainment at home or in public?

In this unit, you will ...

- talk about entertainers in your area, the music industry, and your viewing habits.
- use thinking skills: understand and evaluate.
- read about street performers.
- use strategies to start and keep talking by making notes, asking for opinions, and using qualifying phrases.
- use decision-making skills to plan an event to save a theater.
- design questionnaires for research.

READING

A **Look at the pictures in the article in B. Which street entertainer do you think is the most talented?**

B 3.01 READING SKILL—Identify main ideas **Read the magazine article about street entertainers around the world. Then write 1–2 sentences for each entertainer. Explain what they do.**

Street Entertainers From Around the WORLD

Juan Eze is a street entertainer from Buenos Aires. "Everywhere I go, people always ask me what my **trick** is," he says, "but I never tell anyone the secret of my act. Nobody knows." Juan sits for up to four hours at a time without moving, but he says he doesn't get bored. What's amazing is that he looks like he's **floating**. "Everyone thinks I'm doing nothing, but I'm actually watching everything around me."

Marcel Debard, a fire-eater and acrobat, works on the streets of Casablanca. "I started **performing** about 15 years ago in a circus in Paris. Then someone asked me to help with the fire-eating act and I started to learn how to do it. Is it dangerous? Well, yes, but it's more **dangerous** for the audience. We have to make sure nobody gets hurt. That's why we **blow** the **fire** over the heads of the people."

Huang Jun does a **puppet** show on the streets of Yangzhou, China. "Puppets are popular forms of entertainment in China for adults and kids," he explains. "In most puppet shows around the world, no one sees the person **controlling** the puppets. In Chinese puppet shows, everybody can see everything. It's part of the entertainment—to see how we make the puppets move."

C **Read the article in B again. Match the questions (1–3) to the answers (a–c). Write the letter.**

1 Whose act is the most dangerous? _____
2 Whose act is popular with people of all ages? _____
3 Whose act has the least movement? _____

a Juan Eze
b Marcel Debard
c Huang Jun

D THINKING SKILL—Understand **"Street entertainers are usually very talented." Do you agree or disagree? Give reasons.**

VOCABULARY

A **Match the bold words from the article in READING B to the definitions (1–8).**

1 ______________: doing something entertaining for an audience
2 ______________: a small model character that you move with your hands
3 ______________: an entertaining act that looks like magic
4 ______________: making something do what you want
5 ______________: moving in the air
6 ______________: not safe; likely to cause pain or harm
7 ______________: to push out air from your mouth
8 ______________: flames and heat from something burning

GRAMMAR indefinite pronouns

A Find and underline the indefinite pronouns in the article in READING B.

"Everywhere I go people always ask me what my trick is, but I never tell anyone the secret of my act. Nobody knows."

B Read the sentences and choose the correct option to complete the grammar rules.

Everywhere I go, people always ask me what my trick is.
We have to make sure nobody gets hurt.
Then, someone asked me to help.
I never tell anyone the secret of my act.
Everybody can see everything.

1 *Everywhere* means all places / one or two places.
2 *Nobody* means some people / no people.
3 *Someone* means a specific person / an unknown person.
4 If the verb or adverb is negative, use anyone / someone.
5 *Everything* means all things / all people.

For more practice, go to page 145.

C Read the paragraph and choose the correct option.

Before he became known to **1** someone / everyone / anyone as James Bond, the actor Pierce Brosnan worked as a street entertainer in London. He was training to become an artist, but he met **2** somewhere / someone / something who showed him the art of fire-eating. Soon after Brosnan started performing, **3** nobody / everybody / somebody who worked as a circus agent saw his act and thought it was amazing. Brosnan performed his fire-eating trick on the TV show *Muppets Tonight*. **4** Nobody / Everyone / Everything knows exactly how it happened, but there was a problem with the fire-eating trick and Pierce got serious burns. In true James Bond style, he didn't let **5** anyone / everybody / nobody know he was hurt until the end of the show.

D IN PAIRS How popular are the types of entertainment in the box? Discuss. Use indefinite pronouns.

going to a music concert | going to a sports event | playing board games | watching TV | going to a play | going to the movies | playing video games

A: I know someone who likes …
A: Nobody spends much time …
B: I think everyone likes …
B: I don't know anyone who likes …

SPEAKING

A Think about the street entertainers that you see in your country. Make notes about:

- where you usually see them
- what they do
- how you feel about them
- how you think others feel about them

B IN PAIRS Discuss street entertainers. Try to talk for at least one minute. Use the Confident Communicator box to help you.

I usually see entertainers in the main square. One guy plays the guitar …

CONFIDENT COMMUNICATOR
START TALKING

When you need to talk for a minute or more, try to make notes about what you want to say before you start talking. You can look at your notes as you speak to help you remember what you want to say.

The Music Industry

LISTENING

A **Where can you find good music videos? How often do you watch them? Discuss as a class.**

B 3.02 LISTENING SKILL—Listen for numbers **Listen to this interview with a music producer. Then complete the statements.**

1 Michael Jackson's music video for *Thriller* was ______________ minutes long.
2 *Gangnam Style*, a music video from Korea, became popular in ______________.
3 In 2017, the music video for the song *Despacito* had ______________ billion views on YouTube.

C 3.02 **Listen again. Choose *True* or *False*.**

1 Scott Fleming used to be in a band. True / False
2 He used to be a DJ. True / False
3 Scott Fleming writes songs for bands. True / False
4 Most bands still write their own music. True / False
5 Music videos started an important change in the music industry. True / False
6 Today, anyone can make a music video and post it to YouTube. True / False

D THINKING SKILL—Evaluate **Can a good music video make a song popular? Give examples.**

VOCABULARY the music industry

A **Match the job descriptions (1–8) to the jobs (a–h). Write the letter.**

This person …

1 writes songs for a band. _____
2 is the main singer in a band. _____
3 controls the band's business side. _____
4 makes music videos. _____
5 sings in the background. _____
6 records the songs in a music studio. _____
7 checks equipment so the audience can hear the band. _____
8 focuses on the band's clothes, hair, and makeup. _____

a producer
b lead vocalist
c songwriter
d backup singer
e stylist
f sound technician
g manager
h director

B IN PAIRS **Imagine you could have one of the jobs from A. Which one would you like to have and why? Discuss.**

A: I would like to be a backup singer. You get to sing with different bands.

B: Yeah, that sounds like fun. I like fashion, so I think I'd like to be a stylist.

GRAMMAR *used to*

A **Read sentences from the interview. Then choose the correct option.**

Bands **used to** write their own music.
People **used to** listen to music on the radio.
Did you **use to** be in a band?
People **didn't use to** do that.

1 *Used to* is used for a past action that **is still happening now** / **isn't happening now**.
2 After *used to*, use the **–*ing*** / **base** form of the verb.
3 In questions and negative statements, use ***used to*** / ***use to***.

For more practice, go to page 145.

B **Complete the sentences with *used to*, *didn't use to*, or *did* … *use to*.**

1 Where ____________ you ____________ take music lessons?
2 I ____________ download music, but now I download music every week.
3 ____________ Tom ____________ work in a music store?
4 Those guys ____________ be in a band called Kings and Queens.
5 That restaurant ____________ be a movie theater.
6 My brother ____________ like hip hop, but he does now.
7 ____________ you ____________ watch cartoons when you were a kid?
8 Where ____________ they ____________ live?

C IN PAIRS **Make questions with *Did* … *use to*. Use the phrases below and your own ideas. Then ask and answer the questions.**

- watch music videos on TV
- wear a school uniform
- take music lessons
- hang out with friends at the mall

A: Did you use to watch music videos on TV? *B: Yes, I did. / No, I didn't.*

MAKE IT REAL

You can also use *would* to talk about something that happened in the past.
When I was younger, I used to watch music videos all the time.
When I was younger, I would watch music videos all the time.
Don't use *would* to describe a past state.
I used to live in Mexico City.
~~*I would live in Mexico City.*~~

PRONUNCIATION reduced form of used to

A 3.03 **Listen to the sentences. Notice how the speakers reduce *used to* as /justə/.**

B IN PAIRS **Practice saying the questions and answers. Use the reduced form of *used to*.**

1 A: Did you use to work in marketing? B: No, I used to work in information technology.
2 A: Did you use to walk to the office? B: No, I used to take the bus.
3 A: Did your parents use to own a restaurant? B: No, they used to own a bakery.

SPEAKING

A **How did your parents or grandparents do these activities when they were your age? How do you do them now? Make notes in your notebook.**

- watch movies
- contact family or friends
- do math problems
- listen to music
- take pictures

B IN GROUPS **Compare your ideas. Use the Confident Communicator box to help you.**

A: I think my parents used to listen to CDs when they were my age. I listen to music online.

B: My parents used to watch DVDs. I stream movies online.

CONFIDENT COMMUNICATOR
START TALKING

To ask another person his or her opinion or experience about the same topic, use one of these questions:
And you?
What about you?
How about you?

Viewing Habits

VOCABULARY TV viewing

A Complete the definitions (1–7) with words from the box.

binge-watch channel-surf commercials episode on demand stream TV series

1 ________________ (*adjective*): ready to watch at any time
2 ________________ (*verb*): to go quickly from one channel to another looking for something to watch
3 ________________ (*noun plural*): a set of TV shows with the same characters
4 ________________ (*noun*): a TV program that is one part of a set
5 ________________ (*verb*): to play a video or game using wi-fi without downloading it
6 ________________ (*verb*): to watch several shows in a TV series at one time
7 ________________ (*noun*): advertisements on TV

B Complete the text with words from A.

1 This show is not ________________. You can only watch it on Saturday at 6 p.m.
2 When I don't know what to watch on TV, I ________________ until I find something I like.
3 My favorite TV ________________ is at 8 p.m. every Tuesday night.
4 Did you watch last night's ________________ of *City Hospital*? It was amazing!
5 On rainy evenings, I like to stay home and ________________ my favorite show.
6 There is no wi-fi here, so I can't ________________ that video on my computer.
7 When I watch TV, I often get a snack during the ________________.

C IN PAIRS Think about the TV shows you like and don't like. Say why you like them and how you watch them.

A: I like funny TV series. Sometimes I binge-watch …

B: I stream episodes of a TV series called …

LISTENING

A Look at the pictures. Which one is most similar to the way you watch TV?

a

b

c

d

B 3.04 LISTENING SKILL—Identify opinions Listen to four people talk about their TV viewing habits. Match each speaker to a picture in A.

1 Speaker 1: ______ 2 Speaker 2: ______ 3 Speaker 3: ______ 4 Speaker 4: ______

C 🔊 3.04 **Listen again. Write the speaker who expresses each opinion.**

This person…

1 thinks there wasn't so much choice in the past. Speaker ______
2 says he/she doesn't watch very much TV. Speaker ______
3 likes watching foreign-language TV shows. Speaker ______
4 watches TV shows at the same time as doing something else. Speaker ______
5 isn't interested in watching TV commercials. Speaker ______
6 likes watching things that make him/her laugh. Speaker ______

MAKE IT REAL

To talk about something you like or enjoy doing, use the phrase *to be into*.

I'm really into police dramas. I love them!

D THINKING SKILL—Evaluate **How much time do you usually spend watching TV in a day? How does your amount compare to your classmates?**

WRITING

A Read the text. Underline the three words the writer uses to make contrasts.

I used to watch TV with my brother, but now that I'm older, I stream videos and TV series on my laptop. I rarely watch TV these days, although there are some shows I like. I still watch them, though I don't usually watch them on TV. I watch them online. The only time I watch TV is when I watch soccer on the weekend with my friends.

B Make notes comparing your viewing habits in the past and your viewing habits now.

In the past	Now
shows I watched:	shows I watch:
how I watched them:	how I watch them:
who I watched them with:	who I watch them with:

C In your notebook, write a paragraph comparing your viewing habits now with your viewing habits in the past. Use *but*, *although*, and *though* to make contrasts.

I used to ... but now ...

D IN PAIRS **Share your paragraphs from C. Suggest other ways to make contrasts between the past and now.**

SPEAKING

A Check (✓) all the activities that you like to do.

- ☐ watch TV with my friends and family
- ☐ watch TV alone
- ☐ stream shows on my computer, laptop, or phone
- ☐ watch TV while I'm doing something else
- ☐ watch shows I download on my computer, laptop, or phone
- ☐ watch TV in bed
- ☐ watch only one or two YouTube channels or TV series

B IN GROUPS **Ask and answer questions about viewing habits. Use the Confident Communicator box to help you.**

A: Do you like to watch TV? B: Yes, sometimes. I like watching …

CONFIDENT COMMUNICATOR

KEEP TALKING

Use the following qualifying phrases with adjectives to make what you're saying more interesting:

sort of / kind of really/pretty

My favorite show is a science fiction series. It's kind of / sort of scary and funny.

Did you see the new episode? It was pretty/really good.

Language and Life

Decision-making – Saving a Theater

A **Do you go to the movie theater? If so, which movie theaters do you go to? Do they look like any of the theaters in the article in B?**

B **3.05 Read the article about movie theaters. Then complete the sentences.**

LET'S GO TO THE MOVIES!

Nowadays, large movie theaters (called multiplexes) are everywhere. They have many screens showing different movies. They show 2D and 3D movies. Some show IMAX movies on giant-sized screens. Some also stream live theater shows or music concerts. In addition, some movie theaters that used to sell only popcorn and candy now have restaurants or cafés where you can enjoy a meal before or after the show. Because of competition from TV movies and home entertainment, movie theaters must find new ways to get people back into their seats. Some movie theaters now provide an experience where the audience dresses in costumes or sings along to the music. Outdoor or rooftop movie theaters are popular in some cities in the summer. You can also go to a drive-in movie theater (where you watch the movie in your car). There are about 400 drive-in movie theaters in the US today, although they're not as popular as in the 1950s and '60s.

In the past, almost everyone went to the movies. No one had a TV, so it was an exciting form of entertainment. Many beautiful movie theaters opened in the 1920s and '30s when people of all ages went to see the latest Hollywood movie on the big screen. Some of these theaters, such as the Pathé Tuschinski movie theater in Amsterdam and the Orinda Theater in California, are still open today. However, many of the old buildings that used to be movie theaters now have other uses or are closed.

1 Another word for a large movie theater is ______________.
2 At an IMAX movie, the screen is ______________.
3 In the summer, ______________, ______________, and ______________ theaters are popular.
4 In the US, drive-in movies were popular in the ______________ and ______________.

C **IN PAIRS** **Read the ad from a local newspaper. Then make notes about your answers to the questions.**

DO YOU LOVE WATCHING MOVIES?

Are you between the ages of 16 and 25? Then we'd love to hear from you!

We are looking for young people to help with ideas for our historic movie theater, The Ritzy. Opened in May 1922, it is a fine example of the magical days of Hollywood. Thanks to a large donation of $2 million, we can now make it ready for the 21st century! The Grand Re-opening is planned for the theater's 100th birthday in 2022.

To help with our project, contact us in writing with your answers to these questions:

- What kind of movies should we show?
- What foods and drinks should we sell?
- How much should tickets be?
- What other services should we provide?
- Should we have other events at the theater?
- What popular actors should we invite?
- What other ideas do you have for the Grand Re-opening?

We look forward to hearing from you!
The Ritzy Project Team

What movies to show?

___

___

Other services?

___

___

Eating options?

___

___

Other events at the theater?

___

___

Ticket prices?

___

___

Other ideas for the Grand Re-opening?

___

___

D **IN GROUPS** **Share your ideas. Work together to write a clear, creative plan for the Grand Re-opening.**

E **Discuss the questions.**

1. Were you able to make decisions with members of your group effectively? Why or why not?
2. In what other situations do you need to make decisions about a plan of action with others?

MAKE IT DIGITAL

Go online to find out about a historic movie theater that is popular today. How has it changed?

VOCABULARY review

SCORE: / 10

A Complete the sentences with the words from the box.

backup singer	blow	commercials	on demand	sound technician
binge-watch	channel-surf	dangerous	songwriter	stream

1 I usually ______________ until I can find something I want to watch on TV.
2 I'm a ______________ for the band. I check the equipment to make sure everything works right for the concert.
3 I like to watch ______________. Some are funny, but they don't change my ideas about what to buy.
4 Be careful doing that trick. It's ______________!
5 You can watch many shows anytime. Most of my favorite shows are available ______________.
6 I don't really watch much TV, but I like to ______________ music videos online.
7 One day I hope to be a famous singer, but right now I am a ______________ for one.
8 I ______________ my favorite shows on weekends. One Sunday afternoon, I watched eight episodes!
9 I'm not a good singer, but I'm good at creating words with music. I'm a good ______________.
10 Did you see the street performer ______________ fire from her mouth?

GRAMMAR review

SCORE: / 10

A Complete the sentences with the correct form of *used to*.

1 Did you ______________ work at the music store downtown?
2 I didn't ______________ like classical music, but I enjoy listening to it now.
3 Emile and Isaac ______________ own a recording studio.
4 Did Paolo ______________ be a street performer before he became an actor?
5 My grandmother ______________ have a small black-and-white TV.

B Choose the correct option.

There was an amazing street entertainer that I saw every day on my way to work. **1** Everyone / Anyone watched him, but **2** no one / anyone understood how he did his trick. He looked like **3** nothing / something from a science fiction film because he wore a black and yellow robot costume. He used to stand very still until **4** something / someone walked past him. Then, he moved his body and changed shape until he looked like a small yellow truck. Then, he drove away. **5** Everybody / Somebody who saw his performance said it was amazing.

16–20 correct: You can discuss the music industry and TV viewing habits. You can use indefinite pronouns and the phrase *used to*.
0–15 correct: Look again at the Vocabulary and Grammar sections in the unit.

TOTAL SCORE: / 20

WHAT DO YOU KNOW NOW? Look back at page 27 and add words you know now to the boxes.

STUDY SKILLS DESIGNING A QUESTIONNAIRE

Take the quiz about questionnaires. Go to **Study Skills** on page 129 to find the answers. Then learn more about designing a questionnaire.

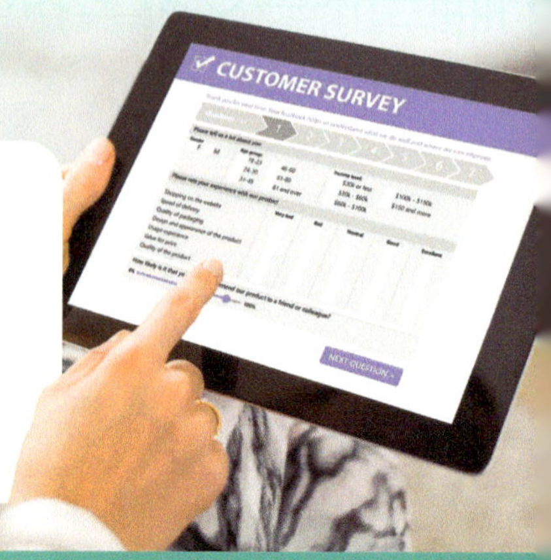

1 The language in a questionnaire should be as clear and simple as possible.
a True **b** False

2 What is the maximum number of questions your questionnaire should have?
a 5 **b** 10 **c** 20

3 On average, what percentage of people respond to surveys?
a 5% **b** 33% **c** 78%

UNIT 4 Your ID

WHAT DO YOU ALREADY KNOW?

1 Think of people you know. Write one word to describe each person.

2 **IN PAIRS** Share and compare your list. Say who the people are and describe them. Add more words to your list, if possible.

Person—Description

DISCUSS & SHARE

VIDEO

3 **IN GROUPS** Watch the video and answer the question.

SYM Are you an introvert or an extrovert?

In this unit, you will ...

- talk about personality types, describe people using superlatives, and compare appearance to others.
- use thinking skills: apply and predict.
- read about personality types in the workplace.
- use strategies to start and keep talking by showing disagreement, describing yourself in the past, and making comparisons.
- use interpersonal communication skills to understand and interact with different personalities.
- follow a school psychologist to learn about this job and the skills needed for a career in education.

Personality Types

READING

A **Think about your close friends. Are their personalities similar to or different from yours?**

B 4.01 **Read this article about different personality types. Then choose the correct option.**

WHAT'S YOUR PERSONALITY TYPE?

Are you friendly and outgoing? Or are you the quiet type? Do you like to work as part of a team or do you prefer to work alone? Psychologists try to understand people by studying their personalities. Read on to find out more about four different personality types.

Type As

Type As are often successful, professional people. They are very organized and focused, and they work hard to succeed. Sometimes, they can be **impatient** with coworkers who aren't as hard-working as they are. They enjoy taking risks, but get stressed easily.

Type Bs

Type Bs are usually **easygoing** and don't get stressed. They love to spend time with friends and have fun. Usually, they're cheerful and **optimistic**. Their worst characteristics are that they can be **lazy** and take a long time to make decisions.

Type Cs

Type Cs are interested in small details and numbers. They are very good problem solvers. They like to be alone and don't always like working as part of a team. They are often **shy** and find it hard to communicate. Type Cs get as stressed as Type As at work. Take time to relax, Type Cs!

Type Ds

Type Ds aren't as optimistic as Type Bs. In fact, they can be very pessimistic. They often worry, see the negative side of things, and get **depressed** when things are hard. They like to feel comfortable and don't like to take risks. However, they are patient and hard-working.

Remember that most people are a mix of these different types. It's unusual to find a person who is only one personality type.

1 Type D people **enjoy** / **don't enjoy** taking risks.
2 Type C people find it **easy** / **hard** to relax.
3 Type B people have a **positive** / **negative** view of the world.
4 Type A people **are** / **aren't** hard-working.

C READING SKILL—Summarize **Complete the summary for Type B people using words from the article in B.**

Type B people like having **1** ______________. They are usually sociable and **2** ______________. They have a/an **3** ______________ view of life, but they can be **4** ______________ and can take time to decide things.

D THINKING SKILL—Apply **Explain what personality type you think you are. Why? How about your friends and family?**

VOCABULARY

A **Match the words from the box to the definitions (1–6).**

depressed easygoing impatient lazy optimistic shy

1 ______________: quiet; nervous and embarrassed
2 ______________: very relaxed; calm
3 ______________: sad; very unhappy
4 ______________: not wanting to work
5 ______________: positive; thinking good things will happen
6 ______________: annoyed because something isn't happening quickly

GRAMMAR *(not) as … as*

A Choose the sentence with the same meaning.

1 Type Ds aren't as optimistic as Type Bs.
 a Types Ds and Type Bs are equally optimistic.
 b Type Ds are more optimistic than Type Bs.
 c Type Bs are more optimistic than Type Ds.

2 Type Cs are as stressed as Type As at work.
 a Type Cs and Type As are equally stressed at work.
 b Type Cs are more stressed than Type As at work.
 c Type As are more stressed than Type Cs at work.

For more practice, go to page 146.

B Choose the correct option.

Because my sister and I are twins, people think we have the same personality, but we are very different. My sister, Danni, is more of a Type A personality. I'm more of a Type B. Danni **1 isn't as patient as / is as patient as** I am. She gets mad about small things, but I don't. In general, Type A people **2 aren't as easygoing as / are as easygoing as** Type B people. Of course, Type B people aren't always relaxed. For example, I'm **3 as impatient as / not as impatient as** Danni when I have to wait in line at the store. We both want to buy our things and leave quickly! Danni and I are different, but we have a good relationship. I think we are both outgoing, and I'm **4 as friendly as / not as friendly as** her. For example, we both like going out together to see friends. But I'm **5 as hard-working as / not as hard-working as** Danni, so I go out more often! I usually stay out with friends longer, and she comes home and does her homework!

C IN PAIRS Compare people. Use adjectives from the reading and any others you know.

brother/sister classmate/friend Dad/Mom Type A personalities/Type B personalities

My brother isn't as easygoing as my sister.

MAKE IT YOURS

Go online or use a dictionary to find more words for characteristics that you and your friends have.

PRONUNCIATION stress on the adjective

A 4.02 Listen to the opinions. Notice the stress on the adjectives.

B 4.03 IN PAIRS Listen and repeat.

1 I don't think swimming is as difficult as skiing.
2 I'm not as cheerful as my best friend.
3 Learning grammar isn't as easy as learning vocabulary.

SPEAKING

A IN PAIRS Play a game of Guess Who. Think of a well-known character from a movie or TV series. Describe their positive and negative characteristics. Ask your partner to guess who it is. Take turns.

B IN GROUPS Talk about what percent (%) of each personality type you think you are. Give reasons. Use the Confident Communicator box to help you.

CONFIDENT COMMUNICATOR
KEEP TALKING

Use the following expressions to estimate:
I think I'm about/roughly/approximately 25% Type A, because …
Off the top of my head, I'd say I'm about 50% Type D, because …
I have a feeling I'm probably mostly a Type B, because …

Teamwork and Personality

VOCABULARY different personalities

A Match the types of people (1–6) to their descriptions (a–f). Write the letter.

1 A leader ____
2 An expert ____
3 A loner ____
4 A workaholic ____
5 A creative thinker ____
6 A risk taker ____

a likes to work a lot.
b likes to be alone.
c likes to try new and sometimes dangerous things.
d is responsible for a group of people.
e has specialized knowledge.
f has new and imaginative ideas.

B IN PAIRS Which type of person from A do you think you are? Which type(s) of people do you like to work with? Discuss and give reasons.

I think I am a creative thinker because I like to think of new ideas. I wouldn't like to work with a workaholic because …

LISTENING

A Do you prefer to work in a large group, in a small group, or alone? Discuss.

B 4.04 LISTENING SKILL—Identify tone Listen to the talk about teamwork and different personalities. What is the style of the talk? Choose and explain.

a serious   b amusing   c critical

C 4.04 Listen again. Choose *True* or *False*.

1 All the members of a team should have the same personality type. True / False
2 A good leader sometimes lets other members lead the team. True / False
3 Many companies have a technology expert on the team. True / False
4 Creative thinkers are often very organized. True / False
5 The information in the talk is only useful for people at work. True / False

D THINKING SKILL—Apply Think about groups/teams that you are in at school, at work, or in the community. Which role do you usually take? Which one do you prefer?

GRAMMAR superlative adjectives

A We use superlative adjectives to compare more than two things. Underline the superlatives.

1. An expert has the greatest knowledge about a subject important to the project.
2. The creative thinker is often not the most organized person on the team.
3. The expert will explain all the most important details to the team.
4. That is the worst mistake you can make!

B Choose the correct words to complete the rules.

1. Use *a* / *the* before a superlative adjective.
2. For adjectives that are one syllable, add *–er* / *–est* to the end of the word.
3. For adjectives that are two syllables and end with *–y*, add *–est* / *–iest* to the end of the word.
4. For adjectives that are two or more syllables, use *most* / *the most* before the adjective.
5. Some superlative forms are irregular: *bad–the worst; good–better* / *the best*.

For more practice, go to page 147.

C Complete the sentences with the correct superlative form of the adjective in parentheses.

1. Diana is ______________________ (creative) person I know.
2. The day I won this award was ______________________ (happy) day of my life.
3. Fernando is ______________________ (tall) student in this class.
4. Esmeralda is ______________________ (talkative) student in this class.
5. The Green Garden is ______________________ (good) restaurant in town.

D IN PAIRS Discuss the questions.

1. What was the most exciting day of your life?
2. Who is the smartest person you know?
3. What is the most beautiful place you know of?
4. What is the worst thing to do on the weekend?
5. (Write your own question.)

____

____

MAKE IT REAL

In spoken English, people often use the superlative to show that something is really good or bad. In these cases, they often pronounce *the* /ðə/ as *thee* /ði/.

That was the /ði/ most amazing meal!

It was the /ði/ worst movie.

SPEAKING

A What were you like in your elementary school classes? Were you the funniest kid? The quietest kid? The smartest kid? The most creative kid?

B IN PAIRS Talk about how your personality changed as you grew up. Are you different now?

When I was in kindergarten, I was the most creative kid in the class. But in first grade …

C IN GROUPS Say how your partner's personality changed as he or she grew up. Did anything surprise you? Use the Confident Communicator box to help you.

CONFIDENT COMMUNICATOR

KEEP TALKING

Use these phrases to talk about changes in your life:

When I was younger / in kindergarten / in high school, I was talkative.

I used to be a little impatient, but I'm more relaxed now.

Until I went to high school / university, I was the shiest person in the class.

LESSON 3 Who Are You Like?

VOCABULARY characteristics

A Complete the sentences with words from the box.

adventurous bossy generous honest rude selfish smart

Someone who is …

1 ______________ tells people what to do.
2 ______________ is intelligent.
3 ______________ isn't polite.
4 ______________ enjoys giving things to people.
5 ______________ loves new and exciting experiences.
6 ______________ thinks only about himself or herself.
7 ______________ tells the truth.

B Complete the table with the words in A.

Positive characteristics	Negative characteristics

C IN PAIRS Compare your answers from B. Can you add any other characteristics?

D IN GROUPS Choose one characteristic from A that describes you and one that does not. Explain.

I think I'm very generous. I love giving gifts. So, I don't think I'm selfish.

LISTENING

A Look at the pictures. Guess how the people are related. Use the words from the box to help you.

A: I think these two are father and son. He's the oldest because …

B: I don't think they're father and son. I think they're …

aunt/niece brother/sister brothers cousins father/daughter father/son mother/daughter mother/son sisters twins

a  ______________

b  ______________

c  ______________

d  ______________

B 4.05 Listen to the speakers talk about who they are like. Then match each speaker to his or her picture in A.

1 Speaker 1: photo _____
2 Speaker 2: photo _____
3 Speaker 3: photo _____
4 Speaker 4: photo _____

C 4.05 **LISTENING SKILL—Listen for detail** **Listen again and choose the words the speakers use to describe themselves.**

Speaker 1: tall / bossy / creative / blond hair / blue eyes
Speaker 2: short / tall / slim / brown hair / blond / adventurous / smart
Speaker 3: brown eyes / small / selfish / brown hair
Speaker 4: bald / tall / easygoing / strict

D **THINKING SKILL—Predict** **As people grow older, do they become more similar to their parents and grandparents in appearance? How about in personality?**

WRITING

A **Read the description of a character from a movie. Can you guess who the character is?**

One of my favorite characters is ______ from the movie ______. The American actor Harrison Ford plays this role. He is a pilot and the leader of the Rebel Alliance. In the early movies, he travels around the galaxy with his copilot, Chewbacca. He's easygoing and very smart, but he is sometimes rude. Princess Leia is in love with him, but she says she is not. They get married in the end and have a son named Ben. I really like him because he's a hero, but he's not perfect.

B **You are going to write a description of a character from a movie, TV show, or book. Make notes about ...**

the movie, TV show, or book ______
the character's appearance ______
the character's personality ______
what the character does ______
how you feel about the character ______

C **Write your description in your notebook. Try to write about 100 words.**

SPEAKING

A **IN PAIRS** **Compare yourself to a member of your family. Describe how you are the same or different. Use the Confident Communicator box to help you. Consider the criteria.**

- physical appearance, e.g. hair color, eye color, hair type (e.g. wavy, straight, curly), weight, height
- your personality
- interests and abilities, e.g. artistic ability, sports, music, career

I'm like my dad. We are both adventurous. But I look like my mom and my aunt.

CONFIDENT COMMUNICATOR
KEEP TALKING

Use the following phrases to talk about who you are like:
I look like/don't look like my mom/dad.
I take after/don't take after my mom/dad.

Use the following phrases to talk about characteristics:
I'm like/not like my mom/dad.
My brother/sister and I are alike/not alike.

Language and Life

Interpersonal Communication – Working with Different Personalities

A 4.06 **Read the conversation. Decide which person has each type of personality.**

Lana: Thanks for coming to the meeting. I made notes on the things we need to do. I think we need to focus on this year's fundraiser and organize it.

Ben: A fundraiser? We tried that last year. You know, we spent a lot of money on T-shirts, and we didn't make any money. I think that's a bad idea.

Lana: How much money did we make? And how much did we lose? Alex?

Alex: I have that information right here. We spent $456 on T-shirts, and we made $153. We had a lot of T-shirts that didn't sell. We also spent $120 on food and drink.

Marta: I think fundraisers are fun! I had a great time at the one last year and I think people enjoyed it. OK, so we didn't sell many T-shirts, but maybe we can do something different this year, like have a raffle or a popcorn stand.

Ben: A popcorn stand? I hate popcorn.

Marta: OK, maybe not popcorn. How about we sell cookies? Everyone loves cookies! I can make some.

Alex: Maybe we should find out how much the ingredients cost and how many we need to make. I'm happy to do that.

Lana: Those are all interesting ideas, but I think we need to focus on two things. First, we need to decide on a date for the fundraiser and second, which person can do which job. I think that would be very useful. Alex, take notes, please …

1 Type A ____________ 2 Type B ____________ 3 Type C ____________ 4 Type D ____________

B Choose the adjective that describes each person.

1	Lana:	organized	easygoing	lazy
2	Ben:	focused	negative	relaxed
3	Alex:	selfish	bossy	logical
4	Marta:	cheerful	pessimistic	honest

C Read lines from the rest of the conversation. Who do you think said each line?

Alex Ben Lana Marta

1 ______________: "I think we should forget about a fundraiser. I don't think people will come."

2 ______________: "These are great ideas. Having a popcorn stand, having a raffle, selling cookies … I'm sure we can make money!"

3 ______________: "We really need to make a decision by the end of this meeting. We can't wait another week. We have to get started as soon as possible!"

4 ______________: "It's good to know how much money we can make. Popcorn is cheap to make, but we can sell it for a lot more money, I think."

D IN GROUPS Prepare a role-play about planning a class event, such as a party or a celebration. Use the suggested phrases to help you.

Student A: You have a Type A personality.
Suggested phrases:
I made notes on …
I think we need to focus on …
First, we should decide …

____

____

Student B: You have a Type B personality.
Suggested phrases:
… is / are fun!
I love …!
These are great ideas!

____

____

Student C: You have a Type C personality.
Suggested phrases:
I have that information …
Maybe we should find out how much …
I am happy to …

____

____

Student D: You have a Type D personality.
Suggested phrases:
We tried that …
I think that's a bad idea…
I don't think people …

____

____

E Role-play your discussion from D for the class. Can your classmates guess who played each personality type?

F Discuss the questions.

1 Did you understand the different personalities better in the role play? Why or why not?

2 In what other situations do you need to interact successfully with people who have different personalities?

MAKE IT DIGITAL

Go online to find a quiz about personality types. Take the quiz and share your results with the class.

VOCABULARY review

SCORE: / 10

A Match the personality types (1–5) to their synonyms (a–e). Write the letter.

1 easygoing _____	**a** happy
2 depressed _____	**b** worried
3 outgoing _____	**c** friendly
4 stressed _____	**d** relaxed
5 cheerful _____	**e** unhappy

B Complete the sentences with words from the box.

expert leader loner risk taker workaholic

1 My best friend is a real _____________. He isn't afraid of anything and loves anything dangerous!
2 I was a _____________ when I was teenager. I didn't want to make friends with anyone.
3 My eldest daughter is a _____________. She works very long hours.
4 Dr. Milagros is a psychology _____________. She knows a lot about how people think and behave.
5 John is the _____________ of this project. He tells everyone else on the team what to do.

GRAMMAR review

SCORE: / 10

A Complete the sentences using *as ... as* and the adjectives in parentheses.

1 Jack _______________________________ as Garth. (not/tall)
2 Emily _______________________________ Marty. (shy)
3 Greg and Henry _______________________________ Barbara. (not/outgoing)
4 Uncle Garth _______________________________ Dad. (cheerful)
5 Raul and his sister _______________________________ Patty. (not/hard-working)

B Complete the sentences using the superlative form of the adjectives in parentheses.

1 My brother is _______________________________ (smart) person in our family.
2 Auntie Jill is _______________________________ (creative) person I know.
3 That was _______________________________ (scary) movie ever! I didn't like it.
4 Martina is _______________________________ (best) manager in the office.
5 Fernando is _______________________________ (young) child in the Perez family.

16–20 correct: You can identify different personalities and characteristics. You can use superlative adjectives.
0–15 correct: Look again at the Vocabulary and Grammar sections in the unit.

TOTAL SCORE: / 20

WHAT DO YOU KNOW NOW? Look back at page 37 and add words you know now to the box.

FOLLOW A PRO EDUCATION

Take the quiz about education. Then go to Follow A Pro on page 130. Find the answers and learn more about education.

1 How many students does the largest school in the world, in India, have?
a 15,000 **b** 25,000 **c** 55,000

2 How much time do elementary school students in China spend on homework each day?
a about one hour **b** about two hours **c** about three hours

3 What is the oldest English-speaking university in the world?
a Oxford **b** Cambridge **c** Yale

UNIT 5

Prepping

WHAT DO YOU ALREADY KNOW?

1 Think about the types of plans or arrangements you often make. Write the words.

2 IN PAIRS Share and compare your information. Add more words to your list.

Events

VIDEO

DISCUSS & SHARE

3 IN GROUPS Watch the video and answer the question.

SYM Do you do one thing at a time, or are you a multi-tasker?

In this unit, you will ...

- talk about making arrangements for a hotel, a school event, and a wedding.
- use thinking skills: predict, remember, and analyze.
- read a dialogue about checking a hotel reservation.
- use strategies to keep talking by making requests and practicing before giving a talk.
- use global competence skills to understand and appreciate social customs.
- learn research skills for school and work.

LESSON 1 Thanks for Your Help

READING

A THINKING SKILL—Predict **Look at the pictures in B and read the first line of the conversation. Predict the answers.**

1 What do you think the customer's first question to the clerk will be?
2 How do you think the clerk will answer?

B 5.01 **Read the conversation between the hotel clerk and the customer. Why is Shiro calling the hotel?**

Clerk: Bonjour, Hôtel Paris.
Shiro: Hello. Uh … Do you speak English?
Clerk: Of course, sir. Good morning. How can I help you?
Shiro: Good morning. My name is Shiro Ito. My wife and I have a **reservation** for four nights starting tomorrow, but we have a problem. Your website says that check-in time is two o'clock, but our **flight** arrives at eight a.m. We'd like to **check in** at about eleven o'clock if possible.
Clerk: We probably won't have rooms before two, but I'll check to see if any rooms might be ready early. One moment, sir … I'm sorry, Mr. Ito, but I can't check you in at eleven. However, I can check you in at 1:30, and I can give you a **voucher** for a free lunch in our restaurant. They have a very nice **buffet**.
Shiro: That's fine, thank you. We'll eat lunch while we wait.
Clerk: Good. We'll take care of your **luggage** at the front desk while you have lunch. I think you'll like our restaurant. The food is excellent, and you won't feel so tired if you have some of our good French coffee!
Shiro: I'm sure we'll enjoy the meal, but I won't have coffee because I want to sleep in the afternoon.
Clerk: I understand, sir. Have a good flight, and we'll see you tomorrow.
Shiro: Thanks for your help.
Clerk: You're welcome, Mr. Ito.

C READING SKILL—Scan **Look back at the conversation to find the answers to the questions as quickly as possible.**

1 How many nights is the reservation for? ______
2 What is normal check-in time at the hotel? ______
3 What does the clerk offer to give them? ______
4 Does Shiro accept the offer? ______
5 Why doesn't he want to have coffee? ______

VOCABULARY

A **Match the words (1–6) to their definitions (a–f). Write the letter.**

1 reservation ____
2 check in ____
3 flight ____
4 voucher ____
5 buffet ____
6 luggage ____

a a lot of food on a table for people to choose what they want
b a trip on an airplane
c an arrangement for something to be kept for you to use later
d bags and suitcases that you take on a trip
e to register at a hotel or for a flight
f a piece of paper that you can use in place of money

GRAMMAR modals of intention, offer, and prediction

A Read the sentences from the conversation in READING B. Label the sentences *P* (prediction), *I* (intention), or *O* (offer).

1 I'll check to see if any rooms might be ready early. ___
2 We probably won't have rooms before two. ___
3 I can check you in at 1:30, and I can give you a voucher for a free lunch in our restaurant. ___
4 We'll eat lunch while we wait. ___
5 I think you'll like our restaurant. ___
6 I won't have coffee because I want to sleep in the afternoon. ___

For more practice, go to page 148.

B Complete the sentences with *will*, *won't*, or *can*.

1 We ___________ probably check out before eleven.
2 I think the weather ___________ be nice tomorrow.
3 I ___________ help you with your reservation if you want.
4 I ___________ have a big lunch because I don't want to feel sleepy.
5 I don't think you ___________ like that restaurant. The food isn't very good.

C Read the conversations and write an appropriate intention, offer, or prediction.

1 A: I can't read the menu because I don't understand French.
B: (offer) ___________________________
2 A: What are you going to order?
B: (intention) ___________________________
3 A: This hotel's restaurant has very good reviews.
B: (prediction) Yes. ___________________________

D IN PAIRS Compare your sentences from C and discuss. Did you have similar ideas? Then practice your conversations together.

SPEAKING

A IN PAIRS Practice a conversation between a hotel receptionist and a guest who is checking in. Read the instructions for each role. Use the Confident Communicator box to help you.

Receptionist: Explain that you have a room on the ground floor near the pool or a room on the 12th floor. Predict why the guest might like each room.
Guest: Tell the receptionist which room you will take and what you intend to do during your stay.

B Role play your conversation for the class or for another pair.

CONFIDENT COMMUNICATOR
KEEP TALKING

Use the following expressions to express intentions and predictions.

Predictions:
I **think** *you'll like the restaurant. / You'll* **probably** *like the restaurant. /* **I'm sure** *you'll like the restaurant.*

Intentions:
I **think** *I'll have fish. / I'll* **probably** *have fish. / I* **guess** *I'll have fish.*

Party On!

LISTENING

A Discuss the questions about parties as a class.

1 Why do you and your friends usually have parties?
2 How often do you go to parties?

B 5.02 LISTENING SKILL—Listen for gist **Listen to two conversations. Then answer the questions.**

1 What are the two conversations about? ____________
2 What are the students celebrating? ____________
3 What do they need permission for? ____________
4 Does Ms. Jenkins give them permission? ____________
5 Which conversation is more formal? Why? ____________
____

C 5.02 THINKING SKILL—Remember **List the party preparations the students talked about in the first conversation. Listen again to check your list.**

1 ______ *the date* ______
2 ____________
3 ____________
4 ____________
5 ____________

VOCABULARY making suggestions

A Complete the conversation with the phrases from the box.

a suggestion	let … know	What about
How about	Let's	Why don't

Jen: OK, **1** ____________ talk about the party. Where can we have it?
Yao: **2** ____________ we have it at Paul's house? He has a swimming pool.
Jen: Awesome! **3** ____________ food and drinks?
Ana: Tony and I can bring food. Could you guys bring the drinks?
Yao: Can I make **4** ____________?
Ana: Sure.
Yao: **5** ____________ asking everyone to bring one thing to eat and one thing to drink?
Jen: Good idea. I'll talk to Paul and **6** ____________ you ____________ about having the party at his house.
Ana: Cool. Text us, OK?
Jen: I will.

B IN PAIRS **Use the cues to write short conversations. Then practice the conversations with your partner.**

1 A: How about ____________ after class tomorrow?
B: I don't know. How about ____________?
A: Maybe. I'll ____________ and let you know.
B: OK, no problem.

2 A: How about ____________ on Saturday?
B: OK, why don't we ____________?
A: Can I ____________?
B: Sure.
A: What about ____________?
B: Cool.

GRAMMAR modals of request and permission

A 5.02 **Listen to the conversations and complete the examples with *can*, *can't*, *could*, and *may*. Listen again to check your answers.**

1 ____________ you talk to the director about that? (formal request)
2 ____________ you design an invitation? (informal request)
3 ____________ I talk to you for a minute? (formal permission)
4 ____________ we use the auditorium for it? (formal permission)
5 ____________ I make a suggestion? (informal permission)
6 You ____________ stay after 10 p.m. (refusal of permission)

For more practice, go to page 148.

B **Number the sentences from the conversation in order.**

__1__ **Zara:** Great news, guys! Ms. Jenkins says we can use the auditorium.
____ **Lucas:** Yes, 10 o'clock is fine. What else do we need to plan?
____ **Mika:** We need decorations. Lucas, can you design some posters to put on the walls?
____ **Zara:** Yes, it's fantastic. We can't stay after 10 p.m., but that's OK, I think.
____ **Mika:** Zara and I will write the text. Mr. Wilson, could you check our English?
____ **Lucas:** Sure. I can do the design, but my English isn't great, so I can't write the text.
____ **Mr. Wilson:** Of course. OK, we have to go to class now.
____ **Lucas:** That's awesome news!

C IN GROUPS **Read the conversation in B aloud to check your answers.**

D IN PAIRS **Find one example each of an offer, permission, a formal request, an informal request, and a refusal of permission in B.**

PRONUNCIATION word stress with modal auxiliaries

A 5.03 **Listen to the sentences. Underline the modal auxiliary if it is stressed. Then practice reading the sentences aloud using the correct word stress.**

1 I can make a cake.
2 May I invite my boyfriend?
3 Could you help me, please?
4 I can design an invitation.
5 I won't have coffee.
6 We can't invite friends.

SPEAKING

A IN GROUPS **Plan a class party. Ask questions and make suggestions and offers. Make notes about your decisions in your notebook.**

B **Describe your plan to your class. You can refer to your notes and the Confident Communicator box to help you. Vote on the best party plan.**

A: We can have our party at …, but we can't …

B: Paula says she'll bring … She's also going to …

CONFIDENT COMMUNICATOR
KEEP TALKING

Remember to use formal or informal language, depending on the situation.

Requests
Formal: *Could you …? Yes, of course. / Certainly.*
Informal: *Can you …? Sure. / No problem.*

Permission
Formal: *May I …? / Could I …? Yes, you may. / Of course. / Certainly.*
Informal: *Can I …? Go ahead. / Sure. / Yeah, no problem.*

Wedding Customs

LISTENING

A Look at the picture and answer the questions in your notebook.

1 How is this wedding similar to weddings in your country?
2 How is it different?

B 5.04 LISTENING SKILL—Listen for main ideas Listen to two friends talking. Then answer the questions.

1 What is the topic of the conversation?
____
2 Are Susana and Jessica both invited to the event?
____

C 5.04 Listen again. Then choose the correct answer.

1 Susana is **excited** / **nervous** about going to the wedding.
2 This wedding is in a **church** / **outside**.
3 The wedding **is** / **is not** very formal.
4 Jessica tells Susana to buy a wedding gift **in a store** / **online**.
5 The wedding and the reception are **in the same place** / **in different places**.
6 Jessica offers to **take Susana to the wedding** / **give Susana directions to the wedding**.

D THINKING SKILL—Analyze In your opinion, why does Susana have a lot of questions about the wedding?

VOCABULARY wedding customs

A Match the words and phrases from the box to the definitions (1–8).

accept an invitation	gift registry	send an RSVP	wedding
dress up	pick up	show up	wedding reception

1 ____________________: a ceremony for two people to get married
2 ____________________: to agree to attend an event or social activity
3 ____________________: a formal party after a wedding ceremony
4 ____________________: a list of things online or in a store that a person or a couple would like to receive
5 ____________________: to wear clothes that are more formal than usual
6 ____________________: to arrive in a place or at an event
7 ____________________: to take a person somewhere in a vehicle
8 ____________________: to let someone know if you are going to attend an event

B IN PAIRS Discuss the questions about weddings in your country.

1 Where do people usually have weddings?
2 Is there usually a reception after the wedding? If so, what happens at the reception?
3 Do couples have gift registries online or at stores? What are some typical wedding gifts?

MAKE IT YOURS

Make a list of words that describe wedding customs in your country.

WRITING

A Read a short essay about American weddings. Then answer the questions.

American Wedding Customs

In the US, some people have very traditional wedding ceremonies, but others prefer nontraditional ceremonies. Many people get married in places like event centers or even at home. Some weddings are in the morning, but most weddings are in the afternoon or the evening. If you receive a wedding invitation, you should send an RSVP. You can do this online if the wedding couple has a wedding website. There is usually an online gift registry so that you can send gifts directly to the bride and groom. Guests at traditional weddings usually wear suits and dresses. People also dress up for nontraditional weddings, but the clothes are usually a little less formal.

On the day of the wedding, the bride and groom do not see each other before the ceremony. In traditional weddings, the bride walks to the groom with her father, but now some brides walk with both parents. After the ceremony, there is a wedding reception, where there's a big meal, and friends and family members give short speeches. There is usually a band or a DJ, and people dance and celebrate through the night with the newly married couple.

1 Where do people get married? ____________________
2 At what time of day do people get married? ____________________
3 Where do people usually buy wedding gifts? ____________________
4 What do guests wear to weddings? ____________________
5 What happens at the wedding? ____________________
6 What happens after the wedding ceremony? ____________________

B Use the questions in A to make notes about typical weddings in your country. Add other information if you want to.

C Use your notes from B to write in your notebook about weddings in your country.

D IN PAIRS Read each other's texts from C. Are your descriptions similar? Compare and discuss.

SPEAKING

A Make notes about another social event you attended.

Type of event ____________________
Location and time ____________________
Clothing ____________________
Ceremony ____________________
Other activities ____________________
Other information ____________________

B IN GROUPS Tell your group about the social event from A. Use the Confident Communicator box to help you.

CONFIDENT COMMUNICATOR
START TALKING

Before you give a talk, practice it. Remember that you can refer to your notes while you are talking to help you remember what to say, but you need to look at your audience, so it's a good idea to practice your talk several times.

Language and Life

Global Competence – Give Advice about Social Customs

A 5.05 **Read the excerpt from a guidebook to the US. Then choose *True* or *False*.**

Social Customs in the US

When you travel to another country, it is important to understand the customs of the country. Here are some useful tips for visitors to the US.

GREETINGS

- When Americans meet someone for the first time, especially in business situations, they usually shake hands. Young people do not usually shake hands in informal situations. Kissing on the cheek is not a common form of greeting.
- At small social events, Americans sometimes greet each person, but normally people say hello to the group in general.
- Use a person's title (Mr., Ms., Dr.) and last name in business situations or when the other person is much older than you. Never use a title with a first name.

SOCIAL EVENTS

- Do not accept an invitation to an event if you don't plan to go. Simply say something like, "I'm sorry, but I have plans that evening. Thanks for the invitation."
- For a dinner party, arrive on time or no more than 5 or 10 minutes late. For an informal party, you can arrive and leave at any time.
- It is typical to take a small gift like flowers or chocolate to a dinner party but not to more informal events.

FOOD AND RESTAURANTS

- In restaurants, Americans often divide the bill so that everyone pays an equal part. If someone says, "My treat," or "I'll get it," that person will pay the bill. Don't argue. Just thank the person.
- If you invite someone to go out to eat, ask if there are foods that they can't eat or don't like before you choose a restaurant.
- Americans often have potluck dinners. This means that everyone brings a large dish to share.

TIPPING

- In the US, the normal amount to tip in a restaurant is about 15%, but 20% is common in a very good restaurant. You don't have to tip in fast-food or self-service restaurants. For groups of six people or more, restaurants sometimes add the tip to the bill.
- It is common to tip taxi drivers about 15%.
- In hotels, tip car valets and bellhops \$2.00 to \$3.00.

1. People often kiss each other on the cheek when they meet. True / False
2. You can use a title with a first name, for example, Mr. John. True / False
3. You shouldn't accept an invitation if you don't plan to go. True / False
4. It isn't important to arrive on time to an informal party. True / False
5. It is common for Americans to share a restaurant bill. True / False
6. At a potluck dinner, you should only eat the food you bring. True / False
7. Most Americans tip about 10% in restaurants. True / False
8. Americans usually tip taxi drivers. True / False

B **IN PAIRS** **An American friend is coming to study in your country. Read the email and discuss answers to his questions.**

New Message

From: jefftheexplorer@usanett.us

To: abl4519@yourcountry.net Cc Bcc

Subject: Social Customs

Wow, I'm going to study in your country! Could you give me some information about social customs?
I have a lot of questions!

- Do people usually shake hands when they meet for the first time?
- Do friends kiss on the cheek when they greet each other?
- If I go to someone's house, should I take a gift?
- If I go to someone's house, should I arrive early, on time, or a little late?
- If someone asks me to go to a restaurant, do they pay, or do we share the bill?
- When do people usually leave tips, and how much?

Can you let me know about any other important customs? I don't want to make mistakes!
Thanks for your help!

Jeff

Send

C **IN PAIRS** **Make notes about any other important customs in your country. Use the ideas below or your own ideas.**

- business meetings
- dating
- gift giving
- holidays

____

____

____

D **IN GROUPS** **Discuss the customs that you made notes about in C and give more information. Discuss any points of disagreement.**

We made notes about ordering in a restaurant. First, we ask what everyone likes or doesn't like. Then each person orders one dish and we share all the dishes with everyone.

E **Discuss the questions.**

1. Did members of your group describe the customs and explain what to do clearly? Why or why not?
2. In what other situations do you need to understand differences in customs?

MAKE IT DIGITAL

Find out about a social custom in an English-speaking country. Write about it and post it on your school's website.

VOCABULARY review

SCORE: / 10

A Complete the sentences with the words from the box.

buffet	dressed up	suggestion	reception	show up
checked in	flight	picked up	reservation	wedding

My best friend got married last weekend, and I went to his **1** ______________. My **2** ______________ to Houston arrived at 3:00 and I went to my hotel. The hotel found my **3** ______________ and I **4** ______________ to my room. I had to hurry because the wedding was at 5:00, and I didn't want to **5** ______________ late! I **6** ______________ in my best clothes. My friends from Houston **7** ______________ me ______________ at the hotel and we arrived a little before the ceremony started. The **8** ______________ was in the same place as the ceremony, and it was a lot of fun. The food was fantastic, but I'm going to make a **9** ______________—if you go to a big wedding, arrive for the **10** ______________ early, because the best food disappears fast!

GRAMMAR review

SCORE: / 10

A Choose the correct modal auxiliary.

Sara: I think the math test tomorrow **1** will / would be really difficult.
Robert: I'm pretty good at math. **2** I may / I'll help you study if you want.
Sara: Great, thanks! **3** May / Will I look at your class notes?
Robert: Sure. **4** I'll / I may come to your house about 5:00 this evening, OK?
Sara: Great. **5** May / Could you bring your laptop?
Robert: Sure. See you later.

B Decide what Sara and Robert are communicating in A. Then write *R* (request), *PR* (prediction), *I* (intention), *O* (offer), or *PE* (permission).

1 ______________ **2** ______________ **3** ______________ **4** ______________ **5** ______________

16–20 correct: You can make suggestions and talk about wedding ceremonies. You can use modals of intention, offer, prediction, request, and permission.
0–15 correct: Look again at the Vocabulary and Grammar sections in the unit.

TOTAL SCORE: / 20

WHAT DO YOU KNOW NOW? Look back at page 47 and add the words you know now to the box.

STUDY SKILLS ORGANIZING TO HELP MEMORIZATION

Take the quiz. Then go to Study Skills on page 131 and learn more about organizing to help memorization.

1 Which do you find easiest to memorize? Rank in order of 1 (very easy) to 6 (very hard).

_____ one word
_____ one word with a picture
_____ a two-word phrase
_____ an underlined word in a sentence
_____ a group of sentences that make a story about a word
_____ a word with a translation

2 Check the techniques that help you memorize new information.

☐ make a song about the thing you want to learn
☐ connect ideas using a story
☐ draw a picture / use color

UNIT 6 Changes

WHAT DO YOU ALREADY KNOW?

1 List five changes in your life in the last year. Include positive and negative changes.

2 IN PAIRS Share and compare your changes. Add more words to your lists.

Changes

VIDEO

DISCUSS & SHARE

3 IN GROUPS **Watch the video and answer the question.**

SYM Do you view change as a positive or negative thing in your life?

In this unit, you will ...

- talk about risk and change, experiences you want to have, and changes in a city over time.
- use thinking skills: analyze, create, and understand.
- read about how people view change in their lives.
- use strategies to start and keep talking by reacting to information or expressing a point of view.
- use collaboration skills to create a list of recommendations for visitors discovering your town.
- follow an interior designer to learn about this job and the skills needed for the field of architecture.

LESSON 1 **Change or Stay the Same?**

READING

A Choose the answers that are correct for you.

I usually prefer to …

1 eat at **the same** / **different** restaurants.
2 eat **the same** / **different** foods.
3 go out to **the same** / **different** places.
4 listen to **the same** / **new** music.
5 go to **the same** / **different** places on vacation.

MAKE IT YOURS

Think of other situations in which you usually prefer to do the same thing or usually prefer to do different things.

B 6.01 Read the article. Do Joe and Elena have the same opinion about changes in their lives?

THE STATUS QUO BIAS—

Why People Don't Like Change!

If you prefer the status quo, you don't like change. You prefer things to stay the same. Psychologists call this the **status quo** bias. Many people have a status quo bias, but some people really like change.

Joe and Elena are both 35 years old, but they have very different **attitudes** about change. Joe has lived in the same city, in the same apartment since 2005. He has been with the same company for 12 years. He hasn't bought a new phone for five years, and he has had his car since 2010. Elena has moved three times in the past two years, and she has had four different jobs since 2012. She has worked in her current job for two years, but she thinks she'll probably look for a new job next year.

There are some **advantages** to the status quo. Life is less stressful in your **comfort zone.** You feel that you are **in control** because everything is familiar. There are no **risks**!

However, it can be a good idea to leave your comfort zone and take some risks. This can help you in your professional and personal life. How long have you had the same job? Are there other jobs that pay better or are more interesting? Do you sometimes feel bored with your living situation or your social life? How many times have you eaten at the same restaurant, listened to the same music, gone to the same places on the weekend? If the answer is "a lot," try making a few small changes. Go ahead, order something different the next time you go to that restaurant!

C READING SKILL—Identify examples Read the article in B again. Underline examples that show the following things:

1 the fact that Joe prefers the status quo
2 the fact that Elena prefers change
3 advantages to the status quo
4 a suggestion for a small change

D THINKING SKILL—Analyze Do you think the writer is more in favor of change or the status quo? Use your ability to infer and explain why.

VOCABULARY

A Match the words from the box to the definitions.

advantage attitude comfort zone in control risk status quo

1 ______________: the present situation, or the way things usually are
2 ______________: a situation or place that you feel good in
3 ______________: a positive characteristic of something
4 ______________: the possibility that something bad or dangerous will happen
5 ______________: your opinions or feelings about something
6 ______________: the ability to make decisions and decide what will happen

GRAMMAR present perfect with *for* and *since*

A Read the sentences and choose the correct answer to complete the rules.

Joe has lived in the same city in the same apartment since 2005.
He has been with the same company for 12 years.
How long have you had the same job?

1 The present perfect with *How long, for,* and *since* refers to …
  a actions or situations that began in the past and continue in the present.
  b finished actions or situations.
2 *For* is used with …
  a a specific point in time.
  b a period of time.
3 *Since* is used with …
  a a specific point in time.
  b a period of time.
4 *How long* means the same thing as …
  a *How much time.*
  b *When.*
5 The present perfect is formed with *have/has* and the … of the main verb.
  a simple past form
  b past participle form

For more practice, go to page 149.

B Use *How long* and the cues to write questions.

1 your family / live in this area? ______
2 you / live in your house? ______
3 you / know your best friend? ______
4 you / study English? ______
5 you / have your cell phone? ______

PRONUNCIATION present perfect contractions

A 6.02 Listen and repeat. Pay attention to the pronunciation of the contractions with *have* and *has*.

1 I've studied English for several years.
2 You've been here since four o'clock.
3 She's lived here since November.
4 It's been very hot outside for two weeks.
5 We've been in class for 45 minutes.
6 They've worked here for a long time.

B IN PAIRS Practice reading the sentences from A aloud. Remember to stress the main verb, not the contraction with *have*.

SPEAKING

A Answer the questions from GRAMMAR B in your notebook. Then think of more questions to ask a partner.

B IN GROUPS Ask each other the questions you answered in A and the new questions you and your partner wrote. Use the Confident Communicator box to help you. Who likes change and who doesn't like change?

CONFIDENT COMMUNICATOR
KEEP TALKING

Use the following words to talk about periods of time.
For exact amounts of time, use *for* six *hours, days, months, years.*
For inexact amounts of time, use *about/almost/around/more or less* six *hours, days, months, years.*

Bucket List

LISTENING

A **Write down four experiences that you would like to have in your life. Tell the class. Find out if anyone in the class has done the things you want to do.**

B 6.03 **Listen to the first part of a podcast. Check (✓) the activities that the speakers want to do.**

- ☐ run a marathon
- ☐ go to Washington, D.C
- ☐ sing at an open-mic session
- ☐ fly in a helicopter
- ☐ drive a sports car
- ☐ act in a play
- ☐ go snow skiing
- ☐ go bungee jumping
- ☐ ride a motorcycle

C 6.04 LISTENING SKILL—Listen for main ideas **Listen to the second part of the podcast. Number the sentences in the correct order. Then underline the two main ideas.**

_____ Your list should include things that you think are possible.
_____ First, try to be realistic.
_____ Thanks for listening, and good luck with your bucket list!
_____ OK, I have a couple of tips for making a bucket list.
_____ Next, don't include too many things on your list.
_____ You probably won't have time to do all of the things on a very long list.

D THINKING SKILL—Create **Write two big things and two smaller things for your personal bucket list. Share your ideas with a partner. Give reasons for your choices.**

VOCABULARY life experiences

A **Complete the paragraph with the past participles of verbs from the box.**

be do eat go hear meet ride run sing win

New Message

To: john2397@outmail.cc Cc Bcc

Subject: Bucket list

Hey, John. I like your idea of making a bucket list. There are a lot of things that I've never **1** ______________. First, I've never **2** ______________ my cousins in Spain, and I've never **3** ______________ to the capital of my country. Those are the big things on my list. There are a few smaller things. I've never **4** ______________ camping or **5** ______________ a horse. Let's see … I've never **6** ______________ Korean food, and I've **7** ______________ that it's really good. I like to sing, but I've never **8** ______________ in public. I've **9** ______________ in a few races, but I've never **10** ______________ a race, so I'd like to do that. I guess that's it. What's on your bucket list?

Send

B IN PAIRS **Discuss which of the things in the email in A you have done.**

GRAMMAR present perfect with *ever* and *never*

A Read the sentences and choose the correct option to complete the grammar rules.

Have you ever flown in a helicopter? Yes, I have. / No, I haven't.
I've never driven a sports car.

1 *Ever* and *never* refer to actions …
  a at a specific time in the past.
  b at an unspecific time in the past.
2 *Ever* is used in …
  a statements.
  b questions.
3 *Never* is used with …
  a an affirmative verb.
  b a negative verb.
4 In short answers to *yes/no* questions, use …
  a the main verb.
  b *have* or *has*.

For more practice, go to page 150.

B Complete the conversations using the present perfect with *ever* and *never*. Then practice the conversations with a partner.

1 A: Have you ________ driven a sports car?
  B: Yes, I ________.
2 A: ________ your brother ever ________ to Canada?
  B: No, he ________, but he's ________ to the US.
3 A: I ________ never ________ an exotic food. Have you?
  B: Yes, I ________. I ________ eaten snake meat.
4 A: ________ you ________ gone rock climbing?
  B: Yes, I ________. It's scary!

SPEAKING

A Complete the questionnaire for you.

Have you ever …	You	Student 1	Student 2
1 ridden a motorcycle or a horse?			
2 been to another country?			
3 made a video and posted it online?			
4 won a competition or a prize?			
5 flown in a plane?			

B IN GROUPS Talk to two different classmates. Complete the questionnaire in A for them. Ask more questions if you want to. Use the Confident Communicator box to help you.

CONFIDENT COMMUNICATOR
KEEP TALKING

To react to information in a conversation, use the following phrases:
Wow! / Really? That's interesting / awesome / really cool!
You've never done that? / You've done that?
I can't believe it!

Changing Cities

VOCABULARY changing cities

A Match the words from the box to the pictures.

bike lane	green space	pedestrian area	shopping mall
food truck	high-rise building	playground	walking trail

1 
____

2 
____

3 
____

4 
____

5 
____

6 
____

7 
____

8 
____

B **IN PAIRS** Which of the features from A are in your area? Discuss.

There are a lot of green spaces, but there aren't many walking trails.

LISTENING

A Look at old and new pictures of Pittsburgh, Pennsylvania. Then answer the question: In what ways do you think the city has changed since the 1970s?

____

____

B 6.05 **LISTENING SKILL—Listen for specific information** **Listen to the radio show *Changing Cities*. Check (✓) the changes to Pittsburgh that Amy mentions.**

They've …

- ☐ built new factories.
- ☐ cleaned up the city.
- ☐ created green spaces.
- ☐ built new high-rise buildings.
- ☐ made walking trails.
- ☐ put in playgrounds.
- ☐ put in pedestrian areas.
- ☐ created bike lanes.

C 6.05 **THINKING SKILL—Understand** **Listen again. Then write one or two sentences that summarize Amy's opinion of Pittsburgh in the 1970s and her opinion now.**

____

____

MAKE IT YOURS

Make a list of words to describe other features of your city or town.

WRITING

A Read the letter to the editor. Decide whether the writer thinks the changes to his city have been positive or negative. Underline examples that support his opinion.

LETTER TO THE EDITOR

Our city has seen a lot of changes in the past 10 years. Some of the changes have been good. The city government has repaired many streets, and they've built new bridges. They've also built a new school and a new hospital.

However, there have been a lot of negative changes. They've destroyed several parks and have built high-rise buildings there. They've built large apartment buildings and condominiums in several neighborhoods, and now the traffic is terrible in those areas. They've taken out a lot of bike lanes, and now we can't ride our bikes on those streets. Finally, they've banned food trucks in the city center, so now there are fewer places to eat lunch downtown.

B Think about the changes in your town. Have the changes been positive or negative?

C Write about changes in your town or city in your notebook. Remember to include several examples to support your opinion.

SPEAKING

A IN PAIRS **Create a combined list of changes to your town and their effects. Use the text you wrote in WRITING C to help you. Decide which changes have been positive and which have been negative.**

B IN GROUPS **Discuss whether the changes to your town or city have been generally positive or negative. If there is disagreement, try to convince your group to agree with you. Use the Confident Communicator box to help you.**

CONFIDENT COMMUNICATOR
KEEP TALKING

Use these phrases to argue your point of view.
It's true that …, but the fact / problem is that …
The city has built / made / created …, and the effect is that …
That's true, but a positive / negative effect is …
Yes, but on the other hand, …

Language and Life

Collaboration – Recommendations for Your Town

A 6.06 **Read the article. According to the writer, what does it mean to be a tourist in your own town?**

GUEST OPINION

Tourist in Your Own Town

By Lynn Williams

I have decided to become a tourist in my own town and the areas near my town. I read an article that said that many people do not know their own towns, and I thought, "That's me!" I've lived here for 15 years, but I always do the same things and go to the same places. I did some research about activities and places in and near my town, and I've made a list of things that I've never done, or that I haven't done in a long time:

- I've never gone to a high school sports event.
- I've been to the history museum only once, several years ago.
- I've never seen the sunset from Pine Mountain.
- There are about 20 restaurants that I've never tried.
- I've never shopped in the farmer's market.
- I haven't taken a walk on the trail next to the river in five years.

Those are only a few of the things on my list. I imagine that it's the same for almost everyone. We all have our routines, and we never do or see a lot of the fun, interesting things near us. So start a sentence with "I've never …" and see how many ways you can complete it. Do some research to find out what there is to do and see in your area. Then, go out and become a tourist in your own town!

B **Choose *True*, *False*, or *NI* (no information).**

1 The writer has lived in her town for a short amount of time. True / False / NI
2 She travels to other countries frequently. True / False / NI
3 She thinks there are many interesting things to do in her town. True / False / NI
4 She hasn't visited the history museum recently. True / False / NI
5 She has visited other museums in the area. True / False / NI
6 She thinks most people know a lot about their towns. True / False / NI

C **Make a list of things that you've never done in your town, or haven't done for a long time.**

I've never been to a high school soccer game.

I haven't gone to the history museum in years.

D **IN PAIRS Discuss your lists. Get ideas from your partner to add things to your list.**

A: I've never been to a high school soccer game.

B: You haven't? It's lots of fun. My cousin is on the team, so I go to all of the games.

A: Cool. Have you ever been to the history museum?

B: Yes, but I haven't been for about 10 years. It was really interesting, so I'd like to go again.

A: Me, too. I think they've expanded the museum and put in a lot of new exhibits.

E **IN GROUPS Look at the ideas on your lists and make recommendations for different types of tourists. Try to think of at least two things to do or see for each type of person.**

Teenagers	Families with young children
Young people on a date	**Senior citizens**

F **As a class, make a combined list of things that you, your family, and your friends can do in your area that you've never done.**

G **Discuss the questions.**

1 Did you successfully match different types of tourists with activities they might like?
2 In what other situations do you collaborate with others to make recommendations?

MAKE IT DIGITAL

Research interesting activities and places in your area. Post suggestions on your school website or social media site.

VOCABULARY review

SCORE: / 10

A Choose the correct option.

Many people do not like to take **1 risks / advantage**. They prefer to stay in their **2 comfort zones / attitudes** because they like **3 the status quo / risk**. There are people who have never **4 gone / eaten** at a food truck, **5 sung / written** karaoke, or **6 ridden / flown** in an airplane. What about you? Have you ever ridden in a **7 bike lane / pedestrian area** on a busy street or **8 driven / ridden** a horse? Have you ever **9 done / gone** camping or **10 won / met** a competition? If not, try something different!

GRAMMAR review

SCORE: / 10

A Complete the sentences with *for*, *since*, *ever*, *never*, or the correct form of the verb in parentheses.

Di: Hey, have you **1** ____________ (see) the new exhibit at the art museum yet?

Jay: No, I **2** ____________ (have, not). In fact, I've **3** ____________ been to the museum.

Di: Seriously? How long have you **4** ____________ (live) here?

Jay: **5** ____________ I was about 10.

Di: You've **6** ____________ (be) here **7** ____________ 10 years, and you haven't been to the museum?

Jay: Well, I've **8** ____________ liked art museums very much.

Di: Have you **9** ____________ (visit) any of our museums? There are several good ones here.

Jay: Yes, I have, but not **10** ____________ a long time, I guess.

16–20 correct: You can talk about life experiences and changing cities. You can use present perfect with *for, since, ever,* and *never.*
0–15 correct: Look again at the Vocabulary and Grammar sections in the unit.

TOTAL SCORE: / 20

WHAT DO YOU KNOW NOW? Look back at page 57 and add words you know now to the box.

FOLLOW A PRO ARCHITECTURE

Take the quiz about architecture. Then go to Follow A Pro on page 132. Find the answers and learn about the field of architecture.

1 The word architect comes from the ... word *architektōn* meaning "master builder".
a Latin **b** Old English **c** Greek

2 The architect Sir Christopher Wren became famous when he designed multiple buildings after London was destroyed by...
a floods. **b** fire. **c** earthquakes.

3 From 1912 to 1948, architects could win gold medals at the ...
a Olympics. **b** Masters Tournament. **c** World Cup.

4 How many years does the typical bachelor's degree in architecture last in the US?
a 3 **b** 4 **c** 5

UNIT 7

Get to Work

WHAT DO YOU ALREADY KNOW?

1 **Think about the career you want and the qualifications and abilities you need to be successful. Write the words.**

2 **IN PAIRS** **Share and compare your ideas. Add more words to your lists.**

Qualifications

Abilities

DISCUSS & SHARE

VIDEO

3 **IN GROUPS** **Watch the video and answer the question.**

SYM Are you born with talent or is it something you learn?

In this unit, you will ...

- talk about career readiness, career alternatives, and employability skills.
- use thinking skills: summarize and analyze.
- read about being ready for a career.
- use strategies to start and keep talking by giving negative answers, expressing doubt, and describing images.
- use problem-solving skills to create a business plan for an entrepreneur.
- learn tips for developing creativity.

LESSON 1 **Are You Career-Ready?**

READING

A What is the difference between a career and a job? Discuss as a class.

B 7.01 IN PAIRS THINKING SKILL—Summarize Read the article. Together, describe in your own words the three main factors in being career-ready.

How Career-Ready Are You?

Have you started your career yet? If you have just started working, you are probably very happy and are learning a lot about your job. However, if you have already worked for a while, you are probably thinking about how to **improve** your career options. If you haven't started working yet, you are probably thinking about what kind of career you want. It is always a good idea to think about the next step in your working life.

First, it is important to understand that being **career-ready** refers to more than training and knowledge about a job or a career. It refers to a combination of **knowledge**, skills, and personal characteristics.

Knowledge includes the academic or technical information that you need for a career area or a specific job, but it also includes other types of knowledge. For example, you may need general math skills or a good level of English.

Skills include specific technical skills, but they also include skills like using your time well, the **ability** to communicate, and working in a team. One of the most important skills today is the ability to **solve** problems.

Finally, you need to understand what personal characteristics and personality types are ideal for different jobs and careers. Some people with excellent academic **qualifications** are unhappy in their careers because their jobs don't really match their personalities.

It doesn't matter if you have just graduated from high school or college, haven't graduated yet, or already have a job; you should take some time to think about your future. How career-ready are you?

C READING SKILL—Understand vocabulary in context Choose the meaning of the words in bold from the article in B.

1 improve
  a make something better b understand c know about
2 career-ready
  a prepared to work b ready to go to college c having skills for a specific job
3 knowledge
  a only academic information b the opposite of *opinion* c the facts you know about a topic
4 ability
  a a fact b a skill c a characteristic
5 solve
  a find a solution or an answer b understand c think about
6 qualifications
  a grades in school b skills or experience you need for a job c hobbies

VOCABULARY

A Complete the sentences with words from the box.

career degree knowledge qualifications skill training

1 Many companies have ______________ programs to teach their employees new technology.
2 The ability to work well with other people is an important ______________.
3 For many jobs, you have to have a college ______________.
4 Primary school teachers have to have a lot of ______________ about many subjects.
5 Good math and technical skills are ______________ for engineering jobs.
6 For a successful ______________, you need a combination of knowledge and skills.

GRAMMAR present perfect with *already, yet,* and *just*

A **Read the first paragraph of the article in READING B and underline sentences with *already*, *just*, and *yet*.**

B **Complete the grammar rules with *already*, *just*, and *yet*.**

1. To indicate that an action happened in the very recent past, use ___________ and the present perfect.
2. To indicate that an action has happened, sometimes sooner than expected, use ___________ and the present perfect.
3. To indicate that an action is going to happen but hasn't happened, use ___________ and the negative present perfect.
4. To ask if an action has happened, use ___________ and the present perfect in a question.

For more practice, go to page 151.

C **Complete the conversations with *already*, *just*, and *yet*.**

1. A: Have you studied for your test ___________? B: Yes, I've ___________ finished studying.
2. A: I haven't read the story for English class ___________. B: I've ___________ read it. It was good.
3. A: Has my package arrived ___________? B: I don't know. Oh, here it is. It has ___________ arrived.
4. A: It's only six o'clock and I've ___________ finished my homework. B: Really? I haven't started mine ___________!

D **In your notebook, write something that you have already done today, something you have just done in the last few minutes, and something you haven't done yet today.**

E IN PAIRS **Ask and answer questions that you wrote in D.**

PRONUNCIATION /j/ and /dʒ/

A 7.02 **Listen and say the words. Pay attention to the sound of the first letter. Then answer: In which sound is your tongue closer to your top teeth?**

yard	year	yellow	yes	yesterday	yet	you	young
jacket	jet	job	John	juice	Julie	jump	just

B 7.03 IN PAIRS **Listen and repeat. Then practice reading together. Correct each other's pronunciation when necessary.**

1. Julie bought a yellow jacket yesterday.
2. Yes, you can have some juice.
3. Have you met John yet?
4. James has just started a new job in New York.

SPEAKING

A IN PAIRS **Make a list in your notebook of any skills, abilities, training, and qualifications you have. Do you think you're career-ready?**

B IN GROUPS **Discuss your lists and decide who you think is the most career-ready. Use the Confident Communicator box to help you.**

CONFIDENT COMMUNICATOR
KEEP TALKING

When we give negative answers, we often add reasons or further information.

A: *Have you graduated yet?*
B: *Not yet. / No, I haven't. / No, but I'm going to graduate this year.*

A: *What have you done to improve your knowledge in social work?*
B: *Nothing (yet). / I haven't done anything (yet), but I'm going to do an internship*

LESSON 2 Career Alternatives

LISTENING

A Discuss the questions as a class.

1 Do you need a business degree to have your own business?
2 In general, do you need a college degree to have a successful career?

B 7.04 Listen to the interview. Choose *True* or *False*.

1	Carmen's business sells food.	True / False
2	The business was very small when she started it.	True / False
3	Carmen studied business in college.	True / False
4	She graduated from college.	True / False
5	She started making ice cream as a hobby.	True / False
6	Customers like the flavor that Carmen has just created.	True / False

C 7.04 LISTENING SKILL—Understand attitude Listen again. Write the words from the box that indicate the speakers' attitudes.

bored excellent fantastic great not interested

1 Carmen's opinion of the ice cream: ______________
2 The interviewer's opinion of the ice cream: ______________
3 How Carmen felt one summer: ______________
4 Carmen's attitude toward college: ______________
5 Carmen's opinion of her sister's idea: ______________

D THINKING SKILL—Analyze Compare how Carmen felt about learning about ice cream to how she felt about learning about architecture. How does motivation help you succeed?

VOCABULARY success

A Complete the text with words from the box.

apply for a job	career path	get a promotion	hires
benefits	get a degree	get a raise	the corporate ladder

The key to success has traditionally been fairly similar for most people. You **1** ______________ and then you **2** ______________. If you're lucky, a good company **3** ______________ you, and you get a good salary and **4** ______________. After working for a while, you **5** ______________, and you usually also **6** ______________ in your salary. If you are good at your job, you climb **7** ______________. However, these days many people do not follow the traditional **8** ______________. Many young people are choosing to be entrepreneurs and start their own businesses. Most do this after college, but some don't graduate or don't go to college at all. There are many different ways to have a successful career.

B IN PAIRS Number the list in order of importance to you. Then share your list. Add more things, if possible.

_____ a good salary
_____ the chance to learn new things
_____ the chance to get frequent raises
_____ good benefits like a company car, health insurance, or long vacations
_____ the chance to get promotions and climb the corporate ladder

GRAMMAR present perfect and simple past

A Match the examples from the interview (1–8) to the descriptions (a–h). Write the letter.

1 We've been in business for five years now. _____
2 When school was out in the spring, I opened the ice cream shop. _____
3 I made the ice cream and she served the customers. _____
4 I made about 20 kinds of ice cream that summer. _____
5 How many flavors have you invented so far? _____
6 I've just created a new flavor called Orange Chill. _____
7 Have you started selling it yet? _____
8 We've already sold out! _____

a an event that happened at a specific time in the past
b an event that happened sooner than expected
c routines in the past
d an event that happened at the same time or immediately after another event
e a question about whether something has happened
f an action that has been in progress for an amount of time
g an action that happened in the very recent past
h an action that began in the past and will continue in the future

For more practice, go to page 152.

B Complete the text with the present perfect or simple past forms of the verbs in parentheses.

Carmen Vega's ice cream shop **1** _____________ (be) open for about five years. Carmen **2** _____________ (take) a class to learn how to make ice cream, and since then she **3** _____________ (invent) a lot of new ice cream flavors. When her shop **4** _____________ (open), only Carmen and one other person **5** _____________ (work) there, but in the past four years, she **6** _____________ (hire) 10 more people. She **7** _____________ (not open) any more shops yet, but she wants to open two more next year. It **8** _____________ (be) a great success so far!

MAKE IT REAL

In American English, people often use the simple past instead of the present perfect:
Did you eat yet? = *Have you eaten yet?*
I just bought a car. = *I've just bought a car.*
I already did my homework. = *I've already done my homework.*

SPEAKING

A Make notes about a person you know about who has been successful with a non-traditional career path.

- Who is the person and what did he/she do?
- Did that person go to college?
- How did the person prepare for his/her career?
- What else has the person done?

B IN GROUPS Discuss the career of the person you chose in A. Use the Confident Communicator box to help you.

CONFIDENT COMMUNICATOR
KEEP TALKING

Use these phrases to express doubt or uncertainty when you answer a question:
Yes/No questions: *I (don't) think so. / Maybe. I don't (really) know. / I'm not sure.*
Information questions: *I'm not sure. / I don't (really) know.*

VOCABULARY employability skills

A Complete the sentences with words from the box.

creative curious flexible honest independent motivated organized

1 If you can make changes when necessary, you are ________.
2 Paul is very ________. He always plans and does things in a logical order.
3 Sandra enjoys working alone. She's very ________.
4 If you always tell the truth, you are ________.
5 Martina works hard and is very ________. She wants to get a promotion.
6 If you have a lot of new, interesting ideas, you are ________.
7 Most children are very ________ and like learning about many things.

B Write the words from A in the appropriate categories.

Types of employability skills		
Intrapersonal (personal characteristics)	Interpersonal (how you interact with people)	Cognitive (thinking skills)

LISTENING

A 7.05 **You are going to listen to a talk called *Getting a Job in the 21st Century*. What do you think the main idea of the talk will be? Listen and check your answer.**

B 7.05 LISTENING SKILL—Identify key words **Listen again. Choose all of the things the speakers mentioned.**

1 In the past, employers usually focused on … and …
   a a high school diploma **b** a college degree **c** personality **d** work experience
2 Someone who is …, …, and … could get a better job than someone with a degree.
   a organized **b** creative **c** interesting **d** motivated
3 In the example, James got the job because he was …, …, and …
   a friendly **b** flexible **c** curious **d** motivated
4 The speaker says that it's best to have … and …
   a a college degree **b** excellent skills **c** good contacts **d** great qualifications

MAKE IT YOURS

Think of characteristics and skills that are important in your career area. Make a list and share it with classmates in the same career area.

WRITING

A **Read the personal statement. Then choose *True* or *False*.**

PERSONAL STATEMENT

I am an English teacher, and I have taught at a language school in Sao Paulo for five years. I have a degree in education from the University of Virginia, but I'm Brazilian, so I know that it's very difficult to learn English! I'm very patient, and I'm good at communicating with my students. I enjoy working with my students and my colleagues. I'm very motivated, and I have just taken some extra courses in classroom management and teaching techniques. I think one of my best qualities is curiosity because teachers should always want to learn new things.

1. A personal statement has information about things like family and pets. True / False
2. The statement gives some information about education and work experience. True / False
3. The statement has a complete list of degrees and work experience. True / False
4. The statement has some information about the writer's personality. True / False
5. The statement is a general introduction to the writer. True / False

B **Make general notes about your skills and qualifications in your notebook. Then use your notes to write a personal statement.**

C IN PAIRS **Read each other's personal statements. Circle any incorrect verb forms. Make suggestions for adding information.**

MAKE IT DIGITAL

When you get ready to write a resume, look up sample resumes and personal statements online. Find one that is appropriate for you and use it as a model.

SPEAKING

A **Many employers say they want employees who are creative. Use basic geometric shapes to create a drawing on a piece of paper. It doesn't matter if you have artistic talent or not. The objective is to think creatively!**

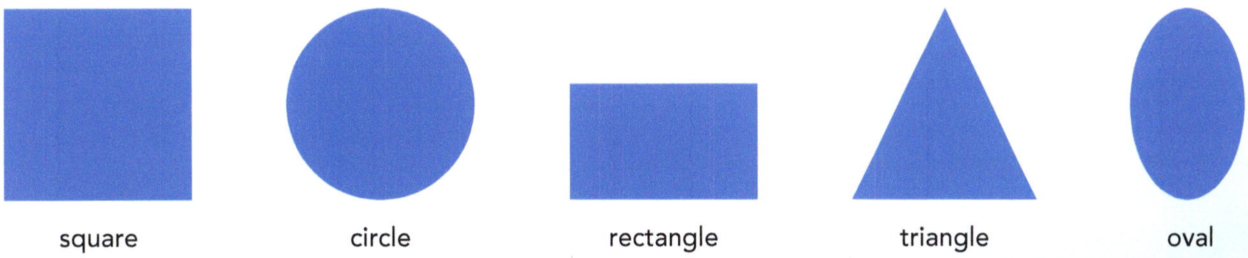

B IN GROUPS **Compare your drawings. If necessary, explain your drawing. Use the Confident Communicator box to help you. In your opinion, who has the most creative drawing?**

CONFIDENT COMMUNICATOR
START TALKING

Describing geometric images:
I've used five circles to create a …
I've put together eight triangles to represent a …
The oval shape is a …
The rectangle and the square form a …

Language and Life

Problem-solving – Becoming an Entrepreneur

A 7.06 Read the article. Then discuss the questions as a class.

1 What is the main characteristic of all of the business possibilities in the article?
2 What specific characteristics and skills are mentioned in the article?
3 What is one of the easiest businesses to start and run? Why?

Turn Skills into Sales

Have you ever thought about starting your own business? These days, more and more young people are doing just that. There are many types of businesses that are not very expensive to start. Often you just need a computer, but you also need to be motivated and patient because starting a business takes a lot of time and hard work.

There are several areas that offer good business opportunities for young people.

- If you are creative, make handmade items: clothes, jewelry, soap, hand-painted T-shirts, origami designs, or greeting cards.

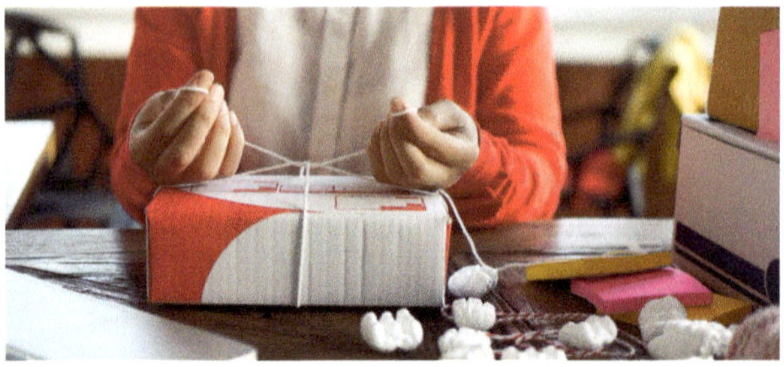

- Are you good at photography? Take pictures and sell them to online stock photo companies. Take photos or make videos of events like weddings, family reunions, or community events. Start a pet portrait business.
- Can you cook? Make cookies or cupcakes to sell to friends, at community events, or online.
- Do you love animals? Think about dog walking or pet sitting. You can also make different flavors of dog treats.
- If you have good computer skills, there are many possibilities for making money. Start a device setup service to help people get started with new computers, tablets, phones, or any other device. Become a tech tutor to teach children or older people how to use computers.
- Do you like public speaking, writing, or performing? If you have interesting things to say, you can start a blog or a vlog and get money from advertisers. Maybe you can become a video personality, or create videos to teach people how to do things.
- Finally, one of the easiest ways to make money is to sell things online. Sell items that your family doesn't use anymore, and buy things online or at garage sales and resell them.

B IN PAIRS **Write three possible small business ideas in the table. Check the criteria that apply to each business.**

Business idea	We have experience in this work.	We know a lot about this.	It isn't too expensive to start.	It's fun.	We don't need a store or an office.
1	☐	☐	☐	☐	☐
2	☐	☐	☐	☐	☐
3	☐	☐	☐	☐	☐

C IN PAIRS **For each business you chose in B, make a list of education, experience, skills, and personality characteristics that you think are necessary for that business.**

Business 1
Education: ______________________
Experience: ______________________
Knowledge or skills: ______________________
Personality characteristics: ______________________

Business 2
Education: ______________________
Experience: ______________________
Knowledge or skills: ______________________
Personality characteristics: ______________________

Business 3
Education: ______________________
Experience: ______________________
Knowledge or skills: ______________________
Personality characteristics: ______________________

D IN PAIRS **Choose the business that you think would be the best for you and your partner. Consider your experience and personality characteristics. Complete the business profile.**

SMALL BUSINESS PROFILE

Type of business: ______________________
Name of business: ______________________
Location (online, store, etc.): ______________________
Products or services: ______________________
Main customers: ______________________

E IN GROUPS **Present your business idea. Vote on the best business idea.**

F **Discuss the questions.**

1 What was the most important part of your decision?
2 In what other situations do you use problem-solving skills to make decisions?

MAKE IT DIGITAL

Do research online about small business opportunities in your country or your area. Share the ideas with your class

VOCABULARY review

SCORE: / 10

A Complete the sentences with words from the box.

apply benefits career curious degree flexible hired motivated raises skills

I have a **1** ____________ from a good university, and now I'm ready to start my **2** ____________. I want to be a nurse, and I think I have the **3** ____________ to get **4** ____________ at a good hospital. I'm **5** ____________ to work hard, and I'm very **6** ____________ about medical information. I like to learn new things. I'm also very **7** ____________ with my working hours. I'm going to **8** ____________ for a job at two hospitals in my city. I would prefer Central Hospital because they have good **9** ____________, like health insurance, and they give **10** ____________ if you do a good job.

GRAMMAR review

SCORE: / 10

A Complete the sentences with the correct forms of the verbs in parentheses.

I'm really excited because I **1** ____________ just ____________ (start) my own business! I **2** ____________ (be) very busy my first week. I **3** ____________ already ____________ (send) about 100 emails to friends, and yesterday I **4** ____________ (put) my new website online. I **5** ____________ (not have) many orders yet, but I'm not worried!

B Unscramble and write sentences.

1 I / my / business online / started / new / just / have / .

____

2 interview / a / gotten / he / yet / hasn't / job / .

____

3 written / you / your / have / yet / resume / ?

____

4 already / my / I've / resume / finished / .

____

5 check / yesterday / I / listings / didn't / job / .

____

16–20 correct: You can talk about success and employability skills. You can use the present perfect with *already, yet,* and *just.*
0–15 correct: Look again at the Vocabulary and Grammar sections in the unit.

TOTAL SCORE: / 20

WHAT DO YOU KNOW NOW? Look back at page 67 and add the words you know now to the boxes.

STUDY SKILLS CREATIVITY

A Take the quiz. Then go to **Study Skills** on page 133. Find the answers and learn more about creativity.

1 **... of people have creative ideas in the shower.**
a 59% **b** 69% **c** 72%

2 **Aerobic exercise makes you less creative.**
a True **b** False

3 **...of people think they could be more creative.**
a 50% **b** 75% **c** 98%

4 **... of CEOs think that creativity is the most important quality for leaders to have.**
a 35% **b** 60% **c** 90%

UNIT

8 Downtime

WHAT DO YOU ALREADY KNOW?

1 Read the definition of *downtime*. Then think of different types of activities you do when you have downtime.

downtime (n.): a time when you are not working or busy

2 Compare and share your activities. Add more words to your lists.

Relaxing activities

Energetic activities

VIDEO

DISCUSS & SHARE

3 IN GROUPS Watch the video and answer the question.

SYM Do you have a lot of downtime, or are you always busy?

In this unit, you will ...

- talk about creative activities for adults, leisure activities for a weekend, and "do nothing" time.
- use thinking skills: apply, analyze, and understand.
- read about "kidults."
- use strategies to repair talking by describing an activity, agreeing with a proposal, and explaining a concept.
- use mindfulness to manage your life and relax your mind.
- follow a resort activities coordinator to learn about this job and the skills needed for the leisure industry.

VOCABULARY

A Label the pictures with the activities from the box.

building a model | coloring | flying a kite | making things with clay

1 

____

2 

____

3 

____

4 

____

MAKE IT YOURS

Find the names of three or more activities that you liked doing when you were a child. Do you still like doing them?

READING

A As a class, discuss what you think the term *kidult* refers to.

B 8.01 READING SKILL— Read for main ideas Read the text. Then match the main ideas (1–4) to the paragraphs (a–d). Write the letter.

KIDS + ADULTS = KIDULTS

a Adults like having toys—no, not boats, sports equipment, or expensive audio equipment, but actual children's toys. They are making things with building blocks, coloring in coloring books, making art with 3D pens, and doing difficult puzzles; they are bouncing inside enormous plastic balls and flying kites. There is a new term for adults who love playing like children: *kidults*.

b Why is this happening? Experts think that in part it is because people, especially millennials, want an escape from the complications of the modern world. Acting like a child is a way to return to a simpler time, but there is another reason for this trend. Doing kids' activities is fun! Why shouldn't adults enjoy doing things like flying kites or coloring?

c People over 50 also spend time doing children's activities. Many grandparents are very healthy and active, and they love playing with their grandchildren. Seniors are playing board games, doing arts and crafts, and participating in other activities that kids love.

d Being an adult doesn't mean that you have to be serious all the time or pay a lot of money for entertainment. Are you creative? Try building a model or making a sculpture with clay. Maybe you love being active, but you can't stand playing competitive sports. Try jumping rope or flying a kite. Find your inner child and enjoy being a kidult!

1 There are two main reasons why young people like being kidults. Paragraph _____
2 Adults are doing many children's activities. Paragraph _____
3 You don't always have to act like an adult. Paragraph _____
4 There is a large group of older *kidults*. Paragraph _____

C IN PAIRS **Discuss the questions. Look back at the text in B for help if necessary.**

1 According to the article, what is the definition of *kidults*?
2 What are the two main reasons that adults like being kidults?
3 According to the article, kidult activities are not necessarily expensive. Which ideas in the article are inexpensive? Which are probably a little expensive?

D THINKING SKILL—Apply **Think about things you like to do in your leisure time. Do you think you are or could be a kidult? Why or why not?**

GRAMMAR gerund phrases as subject and object

A Read the sentences and answer the questions.

a Acting like a child is a way to return to a simpler time.
b People over 50 also often prefer doing children's activities.

1 What is the subject in sentence *a*? ______
2 What is the object in sentence *b*? ______
3 What is similar between the subject in *a* and the object in *b*? ______
4 What form of the verb is used after *prefer, enjoy, can't stand, like, love,* and *hate*? ______

For more practice, go to page 152.

B Look back at READING B. Underline two more examples of gerunds as subjects and two more examples of gerunds as objects.

C Write answers for you using gerunds.

1 Are there any children's toys that you enjoy playing with?
I enjoy making model cars.

2 How can playing with children be good for older people?
______

3 Do you think being a kidult is a good idea for young adults? Why or why not?
______

D IN PAIRS **Discuss your ideas from C.**

SPEAKING

A Make a list of kids' activities that you enjoy or would enjoy doing.

B IN GROUPS **Tell your group the activities you chose and explain why. If necessary, explain what an activity is. Use the Confident Communicator box to help you.**

A: I love playing Hide-and-Seek. It's great because you play with friends, you get exercise, and you laugh a lot.

B: What's Hide-and-Seek?

A: You play in a group. One person is "It." The others hide and the person has to try to find them ....

CONFIDENT COMMUNICATOR
START TALKING

You can use these phrases to describe an activity or a game:
You play ... on teams / in a group / on a field.
There's ... a base / a large ball.
One person is ... "It" / the leader.
You have to ... bounce a ball / run to a base / find the person.

LESSON 2 Plan for Fun!

VOCABULARY leisure activities

A Match the words from the box to the verbs (1–4). Use a dictionary if necessary.

a barbecue	aerobics	jewelry	paddle boarding	to a park
a potluck meal	furniture	kayaking	skating	yoga

Leisure activities

1 Have: a picnic, _______________, _______________

2 Make: pottery, _______________, _______________

3 Do: crafts, _______________, _______________

4 Go: for a drive, _______________, _______________, _______________, _______________

B Complete the online comments with the correct forms of *have*, *make*, *do*, and *go*.

I do all kinds of things that people say help with stress. I **1** _______________ yoga; in fact, I **2** _______________ to my yoga class four days a week. I almost always **3** _______________ swimming or skating on weekends, and I also **4** _______________ aerobics. I exercise a lot, but I'm still really stressed! Molly

@Molly Wow, you need to relax! **5** _______________ yoga and lots of exercise is great, but what about relaxing and having fun? **6** _______________ a craft—**7** _______________ jewelry or candles, or color in a coloring book. I **8** _______________ really bad furniture, but it's fun and relaxing! Jen

@Jen I'm not into arts and crafts, but I agree with Jen. Relax! I like **9** _______________ for a drive in the country or **10** _______________ a picnic with friends. Get together with a group of friends and **11** _______________ a potluck meal or **12** _______________ to a park. Have some fun! Lance

LISTENING

A Take a class survey and answer the questions.

1 How many people usually do more or less the same activities every weekend?

2 What are some of the most common weekend activities?

3 How many people usually plan their weekend activities ahead of time?

B 8.02 LISTENING SKILL—Listen for details Listen to a conversation about weekend activities. Answer the questions. Listen again to check.

1 What activities does Kate describe as "the same stuff"?

2 What does Ken say he does not like doing?

3 What activities do they decide to do on Saturday?

4 What do they decide to do on Sunday?

C THINKING SKILL—Analyze Write the activities from the conversation in B in the categories below. Add other activities to each category.

1 Creative: _______________

2 Cultural: going to a movie, _______________

3 Physical: _______________

4 Social: hanging out at somebody's house, _______________

GRAMMAR verb + gerund or infinitive

A Read the sentences. Then choose the correct form of the verb to complete the rules. Choose more than one option if possible.

I love going out to hear live music.
I like to go to dinner and a movie.
I prefer to watch TV at home.
I prefer doing physical activities.

I'd like to do something creative.
I'd rather do a physical activity.
I would prefer to have the picnic first.

1. *love, like, hate, prefer* + base verb / infinitive / *–ing* verb
2. *would like* + base verb / infinitive / *–ing* verb
3. *would prefer* + base verb / infinitive / *–ing* verb
4. *would rather* + base verb / infinitive / *–ing* verb

For more practice, go to page 153.

B Complete the email with the correct form of the verbs in parentheses.

Hey, guys. Would you like **1** __________ (see) the boat show this weekend? I can get tickets for either Saturday or Sunday. I'd rather **2** __________ (go) on Sunday, I think, because I prefer **3** __________ (do) housework and errands on Saturdays. Also, I'd rather **4** __________ (take) the bus because I hate **5** __________ (drive) in a lot of traffic, and I'd kind of prefer **6** __________ (get) there early. What do you think? Does all of that sound OK?

PRONUNCIATION *–ould* words

A 8.03 Listen to the conversation and answer the questions.

Omar: Would you like to go to the new museum tomorrow?
Jamal: That sounds great. We should go early, when there are fewer people.
Omar: Actually, I would rather go in the afternoon. Is that OK?
Jamal: That's fine. Could you pick me up?
Omar: Sure.

1. Do *would*, *should*, and *could* have the same vowel sound or different sounds?
2. Do you hear the *l* in *would*, *should*, and *could*?

B IN PAIRS Practice the conversation. Pay special attention to the pronunciation of *would*, *should*, and *could*.

MAKE IT REAL

Although the meaning of *hate*, *like*, *love*, and *prefer* is the same when used with an infinitive or with a gerund, the infinitive form is more commonly used in American English than the gerund form.

SPEAKING

A IN PAIRS In your notebook, make a list of activities that you can do in your area in each category.

- Creative
- Cultural
- Physical
- Social

B IN GROUPS Compare your lists from A. Create one list of activities that you all like doing.

C IN GROUPS Discuss activities for a group activity weekend. Use the Confident Communicator box to help you.

A: I love / like / don't really like / can't stand … *B: I would like to / prefer to / rather …*

CONFIDENT COMMUNICATOR
KEEP TALKING

Agreeing with a proposal
Sure. / That's fine with me. / That sounds good.

Objecting to a proposal
The problem is that … / Sorry, but I don't really like … / Unfortunately, I can't …

Is It OK to Do Nothing?

LISTENING

A **Do you enjoy doing nothing? Why or why not? Discuss as a class.**

B 8.04 LISTENING SKILL—Listen for reasons **Listen to a class discussion and check (✓) the reasons you hear for and against doing nothing.**

For
- ☐ It's fun.
- ☐ It helps you relax.
- ☐ It helps you be more creative.
- ☐ It helps you solve problems.

Against
- ☐ It's boring.
- ☐ It makes you tired.
- ☐ It makes you feel guilty.
- ☐ It's unhealthy.

C THINKING SKILL—Understand **List the examples of activities that are classified as *doing nothing* in the class discussion from B. Add several more examples of activities that you consider to be *doing nothing*.**

____

____

____

____

VOCABULARY adjectives of feeling

A **Match the words from the box to the definitions (1–5).**

bored guilty nervous rested stressed

1. ______________: worried or a little scared
2. ______________: not interested in the activity or conversation
3. ______________: feeling bad because you are doing something wrong
4. ______________: worried about professional, financial, or personal problems
5. ______________: not tired

B IN PAIRS **Ask and answer the questions.**

1. How do you feel when you do nothing?
2. What situations make you feel nervous?
3. What do you do if you feel stressed?
4. When do you get bored?

A: I feel bored when I do nothing.

B: I eat when I feel stressed.

WRITING

A Read the blog entry. Then answer the questions.

MY PROFILE

Some people say that it's good to do nothing, but I disagree. I think doing nothing is bad for you. First, most people think that doing nothing is not productive, and I agree. It's better to use your time studying, working, or helping other people. Second, some people say that doing nothing helps you think creatively and solve problems. However, when people say they are doing nothing, they are usually doing things like looking at social media or watching TV. Those activities don't help you think creatively or solve problems. Finally, the main problem is that doing nothing can become a habit. If you take a break to relax and do nothing, it is difficult to start working or studying again. It is easier if you finish working or studying before you take a break.

1 How many reasons does the writer give to support his argument? ____________

2 What words does the writer use to indicate that he is introducing a new point? ____________

3 Where does the writer place his most important argument? ____________

B In your opinion, is it good or bad to do nothing? Think about the question and make notes in your notebook.

C Use your notes from B to write a blog entry in your notebook.

D IN PAIRS Exchange papers with someone who has the opposite opinion from yours. Read each other's blog entries and then discuss the question.

Did your partner's arguments change your opinion?

SPEAKING

A Make notes on the questions.

1 How often do you do nothing?

____

____

2 When you do nothing, what do you do?

____

____

B IN GROUPS Compare your ideas. Say what the perfect do-nothing day would be for you. Use the Confident Communicator box to help you.

A: On a do-nothing day, I'd like to …

B: Really? I'd rather …

CONFIDENT COMMUNICATOR
START TALKING

Explaining a concept

Doing nothing **means** *sitting around just thinking about things.*

To me, *doing nothing* **is** *reading a good book and not going out.*

For me, *the perfect do-nothing day is sitting/going/having …*

I think *doing nothing* **is** *when you …*

Language and Life

Mindfulness – Relaxing Your Mind

A 8.05 **IN PAIRS** **Read the article. Then discuss the questions.**

MINDFULNESS FOR MENTAL RELAXATION

Study, work, family, friends, pets, social media ... We feel tired and stressed because we can't do everything. The effects of this are that we are less efficient, less creative, and less happy. We all try to do leisure activities like playing sports or watching movies, but what about leisure time for the mind?

In recent years, many people have started to practice *mindfulness*. Being mindful means that you are paying attention to what you are doing at the moment, to your feelings, and to the things that are happening around you. You are not thinking about things that have already happened or worrying about what is going to happen. For example, if you notice how the sun feels on your face, or how your clean clothes smell, you are being mindful.

There are some simple things that you can do to practice mindfulness. Do you like walking? Go for a walk, but don't think about walking fast or going a certain distance. Walk slowly. Think about how your body feels. Stop and look at trees or flowers. Stop and close your eyes. What do you hear, feel, or smell? Would you rather do something creative? Paint something or do a craft. Don't worry if it isn't good. Think about the process. How does the paintbrush feel in your hand? What does each color make you think of? Giving your brain time to relax can help you feel less stressed and more rested. The result is more creativity and better problem solving.

1 What are the effects of being tired and stressed?
2 What is mindfulness?
3 How is a mindful activity different from the normal way we do things?
4 What are the effects of giving your brain time to relax?

B Choose one of the mindfulness activities and try it.

Positive reflection (5 minutes)

1 Think of three things that you are thankful for and write them down.
2 Think of three good things that you have done or that have happened to you this week and write them down.
3 Close your eyes. Breathe slowly. Take a few minutes to reflect on the things on your lists. How do you feel?

Observation (5 minutes)

1 Go to a window in your classroom. If there are no windows, choose an area of your classroom to focus on.
2 Look at everything you see. Don't think about the names of the things at all. Notice shapes and colors.
3 Notice changes in the light or movement of the objects.
4 If you start thinking about other things, notice a color or a shape again. Focus only on that color or shape.

Visualization (5 minutes)

1 Think of a place that you love. Close your eyes and imagine that you are in that place.
2 Think about what is around you. For example, if you are in the mountains, what do you see? Are there tall trees? Is there snow on the mountains? Is the grass green?
3 Use your other senses. What do you smell? Flowers? What do you hear? Birds singing? A waterfall? What do you feel? The sun? A cool wind on your skin?
4 Breathe slowly and relax. If you start thinking about other things, focus on the details of the place.

C IN GROUPS Discuss your experience. Use the questions as a guide.

1 Which activity did you choose?
2 Was it easy or hard to do the activity?
3 How do you feel after the activity?
4 Did you like doing the activity?
5 Do you think mindfulness activities can help your mind relax when you are feeling stressed?

D IN PAIRS Choose a situation and suggest a mindfulness activity to help the person feel less stressed. You can use an activity from B or invent your own activity.

1 Paul is very nervous about a big exam tomorrow. He's at home, and he's trying to study, but he can't concentrate. He's messaging friends on social media and saying that he thinks the exam will be very hard.
2 Sam is worried about his health. He knows that he doesn't always eat well and he doesn't sleep enough. When he worries, he eats junk food and watches TV very late at night. He says that junk food and action movies make him feel happy!
3 Kathy is on the bus, on her way to her university classes. There is a lot of traffic, and the bus is going very slowly. Kathy is really bored, and she is getting angry because she's probably going to be late for class.

E IN GROUPS Share your mindfulness activity from D with your group. Then discuss the questions.

1 Have you ever been in any of the situations in **D**? How did you feel? What did you do?
2 Of the ideas that you heard, which activities would you prefer to do?

F Discuss the questions.

1 Was it useful to take time to relax? Why or why not?
2 What other ways do you use to calm yourself?

MAKE IT DIGITAL

Do research to find more mindfulness activities. Choose one or two and try them. Use questions 1–5 from **C** to report to your class about the activities you did.

VOCABULARY review

SCORE: / 10

A Complete the sentences with the words in the box.

kite coloring potluck crafts model skating

1 We're going to have a big ____________ meal. Everyone is going to bring a different dish.
2 My dad's hobby is building ____________ airplanes.
3 It's windy today – a great day for flying a ____________.
4 It's a nice day. Let's go ____________ in the park.
5 I do a lot of different ____________. It's relaxing and creative.
6 I love ____________ pictures. I usually use colored pencils.

B Choose the correct option.

1 I'm worried about work because I have too much to do. I'm really **bored / guilty / stressed**.
2 I'm not doing anything, and my friends are all busy. I'm **bored / stressed / rested**.
3 I had a great weekend. I saw friends and slept a lot. I feel very **guilty / bored / rested**.
4 My brother didn't invite his friend Joe to the party. Now he feels **stressed / guilty / nervous**.

GRAMMAR review

SCORE: / 10

A Complete the email with the correct form of the verbs in parentheses.

Hey, Susie. You love **1** ____________ (do) crafts, right? I'm taking a cool art class. We're learning to create art with different materials. I don't like **2** ____________ (paint) or **3** ____________ (draw), but **4** ____________ (make) models or clay sculptures is really fun! Also, we're, **5** ____________ (make) cool jewelry out of paper. Would you like **6** ____________ (go) to a class with me? Is Monday OK, or would you prefer **7** ____________ (go) on Wednesday? I'd rather **8** ____________ (take) you on Monday if possible. I think you'll like **9** ____________ (visit) the class, and I'm sure you'd rather **10** ____________ (go) to an art class than study for the math exam. 🙂

16–20 correct: You can discuss leisure activities and use adjectives of feeling. You can use gerunds.
0–15 correct: Look again at the Vocabulary and Grammar sections in the unit.

TOTAL SCORE: / 20

WHAT DO YOU KNOW NOW? Look back at page 77 and add the words you know now to the boxes.

FOLLOW A PRO LEISURE

Take the quiz about activities coordinators. Then go to **Follow A Pro** on page 134. Find the answers and learn more about the leisure industry.

1 In the US, the average annual salary for activities coordinators is about …
a $12,000. **b** $22,000. **c** $32,000.

2 … is NOT usually a requirement for an activities coordinator.
a Physical fitness **b** Teaching experience **c** Public speaking experience

3 Choose all that are true. Activities coordinators work …
a at schools. **b** at resort hotels. **c** on cruise ships. **d** at senior homes. **e** at camps.

UNIT 9

Room for Me

WHAT DO YOU ALREADY KNOW?

1 Think about where you live. Is it a house, an apartment, or something else? Write words that describe your home and what's in it.

2 **IN PAIRS** Share and compare your information. Add more words to your list.

Furniture

Parts of a house/rooms

VIDEO

DISCUSS & SHARE

3 **IN GROUPS** Watch the video and answer the question.

SYM Would you prefer to live in a house or an apartment?

In this unit, you will ...

- talk about different kinds of housing, where you prefer to live, and what houses will be like in the future.
- use thinking skills: understand and evaluate.
- read about housing solutions.
- use strategies to keep talking by asking for and giving opinions.
- use decision-making skills to plan and develop a neighborhood.
- learn tips for problem solving in group work.

READING

A READING SKILL—Predict **Look at the picture and the title of the article in B. What do you think the article is about?**

B 9.01 **Read the article. Then check (✓) the correct options.**

Half-houses in Chile

In many areas, people can't **afford** to buy or **rent** a place to live. It's a problem that will become worse in the future. Some cities have found interesting solutions.

One example is half-houses in Chile. An earthquake hit the town of Constitución in 2010 and destroyed about 80% of the buildings. The local government hired an architecture firm to provide **low-cost** houses. They built houses that are only half-finished. The owners finish the house when they have the money. It means that each family can decide what they need: a garage, another bedroom, a **hall**, a **balcony**. One resident says: "We're going to build another bedroom and bathroom in two years. We can add our personal style."

Another solution is micro-units, like those at Carmel Place in New York City. These are very small apartments, around 28 square meters. They are too small for a family, but perfect for single young professionals. Each one-room apartment has the usual appliances—a stove, a refrigerator, and a microwave—and there's a room in another part of the building for washing clothes. The smart use of special furniture means the room can become a bedroom, kitchen, office, or living room. The desk becomes a dining table and the couch becomes a bed. The coffee table folds down and goes under the bed at night. A young resident says: "I'm having a friend over for dinner tonight. I just turn the bed into a **couch**, the desk into a table, and we're good to go!"

1 What are the advantages of half-houses for the city?

- ☐ They are low-cost.
- ☐ They don't collapse in an earthquake.
- ☐ They are big enough for families.
- ☐ They have a garage.
- ☐ Residents choose what to build.
- ☐ The half-houses are built in a traditional style.

2 What are the apartments like at Carmel Place?

- ☐ People can change the small space in many ways.
- ☐ They are big enough for families.
- ☐ They have a kitchen and an office in two rooms.
- ☐ There are washing machines in the apartment building.

C THINKING SKILL—Understand **Compare these examples to your own area. What housing programs does your area offer? Do people use these programs?**

VOCABULARY

A Complete each sentence with a bold word from the text in READING B.

1 Something that is ______________ is cheap, not expensive.
2 A ______________ is a place where you can stand outside a window.
3 If you can ______________ something, you have enough money for it.
4 A ______________ is a seat for two or three people.
5 The long, narrow area in a house that leads to different rooms is the ______________.
6 When you ______________ a place, you pay money each month to live there.

MAKE IT REAL

When people say they are "good to go," it means they are ready to do something, e.g. *We have popcorn, soda, and tickets for the movie. We're good to go!*

GRAMMAR future forms

A Read the article in READING B again. Underline sentences with *will*, *going to*, and the present progressive. Then read the sentence below and write if it refers to the present or the future.

1 My train leaves at nine o'clock tomorrow morning. ____________

B Complete the grammar rules with words from the box.

arrangements intentions predictions schedule

1 To make ____________ about the future, we use *will* or *going to*.
2 To talk about future ____________, we use *going to*.
3 To talk about future ____________, we use the present progressive.
4 To talk about future events that happen on a ____________, we use the simple present.

For more practice, go to page 154.

C Choose the correct option.

1 I rent / 'm going to rent an apartment downtown next year.
2 I meet / am meeting my friend tomorrow at 9 a.m.
3 Do you think you will rent / are renting an apartment in the future?
4 What do you do / are you going to do this weekend?
5 My new job starts / will starting next month, and I need to find somewhere to live.

D IN PAIRS Ask and answer the questions.

1 What fun things are you doing this week?
2 What are you going to do this weekend?
3 When does your next vacation start? What are you going to do?

SPEAKING

A Check (✓) the housing problems your neighborhood or city faces. Then add more ideas.

- ☐ Rents are high.
- ☐ Houses/apartments are expensive.
- ☐ There aren't enough places to live.
- ☐ The construction isn't good.
- ☐ Houses/apartments are too small.
- ☐ ____________

B How do you think your neighborhood or city is going to change over the next five years? Choose if you *Agree* or *Disagree*. Add two more ideas.

1 Companies or the government are going to build many more houses or apartment buildings. Agree / Disagree
2 Young people will move to other areas to live. Agree / Disagree
3 Companies or the government will build cheaper places to live. Agree / Disagree
4 ____________ Agree / Disagree
5 ____________ Agree / Disagree

C IN PAIRS Discuss the questions. Use the Confident Communicator box to help you.

1 What are some problems with housing in your area?
2 How do you think housing will change in your area?

CONFIDENT COMMUNICATOR
KEEP TALKING

Use the following expressions to ask for opinions.

What do you think? *What about you?*
What's your opinion? *Do you agree?*

LESSON 2 I Might Live Downtown

VOCABULARY living together

A Complete the sentences with words from the box.

apartment hunting	live alone	roommate	share the chores
housemate	rent a room	share the bills	studio apartment

1 I'm going to go __________ this afternoon. I want to find a place to live.
2 You share a house with a __________, but you share a room or an apartment with a __________.
3 You __________ if you don't live with other people.
4 When you live in a house that you share with other people, you __________ in a house.
5 When people __________ and __________, they pay for things together, and they take turns doing the chores.
6 A __________ is an apartment with one room and a bathroom.

MAKE IT YOURS

Do you live in an apartment, a house, or a townhouse? Search online or use a dictionary to find the right words and phrases.

B IN PAIRS Would you rather live alone or have roommates? Discuss. Explain why using the phrases from A.

LISTENING

A 9.02 LISTENING SKILL—Listen for attitude Listen to two people talking. Choose the word that describes each person's attitude.

1 Ashley: **a** uncertain **b** afraid **c** unhappy
2 Ethan: **a** nervous **b** excited **c** uninterested

B 9.02 Listen again and choose the correct option.

1 Ashley … living with her family.
a likes **b** doesn't like
2 Ethan's brother and his friends …
a share an apartment. **b** live near each other.
3 Ashley … to live with a friend.
a wants **b** doesn't want
4 Ethan says that … might be hard.
a finding a cheap apartment **b** traveling to work

C THINKING SKILL—Evaluate What are the advantages and disadvantages of living with a friend?

PRONUNCIATION /aʊ/ and /oʊ/

A 9.03 Write each word in the correct category. Then listen and repeat the words.

allow	found	know	own
sound	below	now	phone

1 /aʊ/ like *house*: __________ __________ __________ __________
2 /oʊ/ like *go*: __________ __________ __________ __________

GRAMMAR future possibility and certainty

A Read the sentences. Then choose the correct option.

I **might** still be at home with Mom and Dad.
You **could** live with a friend.
You **may** find something cheap outside the city.
I **probably won't** have enough money for that.
I **will definitely** miss them!

1 We use *may*, *might*, and *could* to talk about things that are **sure** / **possible** in the future.
2 We use *probably* when we are not **sure** / **almost** sure about the future.
3 We use *definitely* when we are **not sure** / **very sure** about the future.

For more practice, go to page 155.

B Read the conversations and choose the correct option.

1 A: Do you think you might live in your home town after you graduate?
B: Oh, yes! I ______________ live there. I'm sure of that.
a probably will **b** might **c** will definitely

2 A: Do you think you'll live in another city in the future?
B: Maybe, but I ______________. I'm not sure.
a might not **b** could not **c** won't

3 A: Do you think you might live in another country one day?
B: Well, I guess I ______________ get a job in another country. I don't know.
a will **b** may not **c** could

4 A: What kind of place do you think you might live in after you graduate?
B: I ______________ have enough money for a house, so I might rent a small apartment.
a may not **b** could not **c** might

C IN PAIRS Talk about future possibilities. Finish the sentences and ask each other questions.

1 This evening, I might … 2 Tomorrow, I may … 3 This weekend, I'll probably …

SPEAKING

A Rate how likely each possibility is for you in the future: 1 (*definitely won't*), 2 (*probably won't*), 3 (*may, might, could*), 4 (*probably will*), or 5 (*definitely will*).

live in a small town _____
live in another country _____
live in the center of a big city _____
live in a house with a yard _____
live with your parents _____
live with other family members _____
live in an apartment building _____
live with a friend _____

B IN PAIRS Talk about where you might live in the future. Ask questions about your predictions. Use the Confident Communicator box to help you.

A: I'll probably live in another country for a few years. *B: Why is that?*
A: I might get a job and …

CONFIDENT COMMUNICATOR
KEEP TALKING

Use the following expressions to ask for reasons for opinions.
Why is that?
Why do you think that?
Why do you say that?

LESSON 3 The Future of Houses

VOCABULARY appliances

A **IN PAIRS** **Choose the three things you think might change most in the future. Discuss how you think they might change.**

air conditioner

dishwasher

solar panel

lighting

kitchen stove

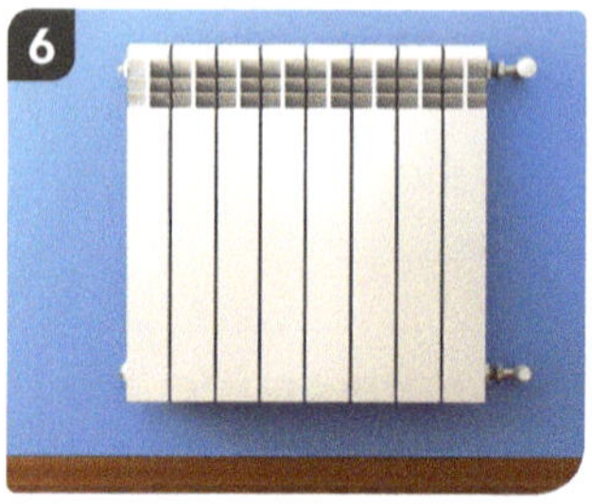

heater

washing machine

B **IN PAIRS** **Discuss the question and check the meanings of the words and phrases in bold.**

How can **sunlight** help us **save energy** and **save money**?

LISTENING

A **You are going to listen to a talk. Look at the picture and say what you think the talk is about.**

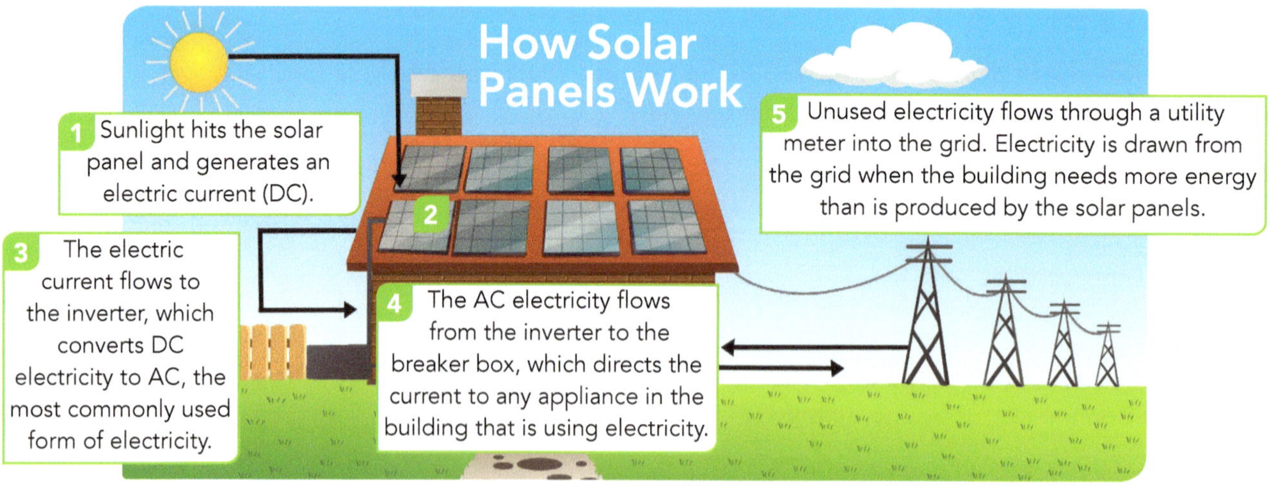

B 9.04 LISTENING SKILL—Take notes **Listen to a talk and complete the notes.**

solar panels

- receive **1** ______________ on sunny days
- create **2** ______________ from special materials

inverter

- takes DC current from the **3** ______________
- sends AC current to the **4** ______________

electricity grid

- takes electricity that the house **5** ______________
- provides power when there is **6** ______________

C THINKING SKILL—Evaluate **How can we persuade more people to use solar power?**

WRITING

A Read the article and answer the question.

Future Homes

What will the homes of tomorrow be like? I think we'll see big changes in entertainment. For example, homes will have 3D movie theaters with amazing sound. We might have virtual reality in some homes. I don't think that will be very popular because it will be expensive. There could also be big changes in the kitchen. For instance, you might choose a recipe and the stove will know how to cook it. It will tell you when your food is ready. Finally, parts of your house will change. Take windows, for example. They might go dark automatically at night to help you sleep. Or the windows might show messages to people at your door. Houses are going to change in many ways, and I can't wait!

According to the writer, what changes might we see in entertainment, in kitchens, and in windows?

____

B Choose the correct option.

1 The way we use energy will change. As / For example, all houses will have solar panels.
2 Rooms will change. One / For instance, houses might have a special room just for virtual reality.
3 Some rooms will change. Take / Look bathrooms, for example. We will use much less water.

C Choose three things you think are going to be different in our homes. In your notebook, write the main way you think each one is going to be different.

robots: They will clean our homes.

D Write a paragraph about how you think houses might change in the future.

E IN PAIRS Share your paragraphs from D. Comment on the way your partner uses examples.

MAKE IT DIGITAL

Search online for ideas on homes of the future. Tell the class what you find.

SPEAKING

A Check (✓) the future changes in homes that you are interested in. Add your own ideas.

- ☐ robots in the home
- ☐ virtual reality
- ☐ entertainment
- ☐ use of energy
- ☐ use of water
- ☐ security

______________________ ______________________

B IN PAIRS Talk about the things that interest you about the future of homes. Give reasons for your opinions. Use the Confident Communicator box to help you.

CONFIDENT COMMUNICATOR
KEEP TALKING

Use the following expressions to give reasons for your opinions.
I think we'll have robots in the home because they can do housework for us.
The reason for that is robots will do housework for us.
That's because robots will do housework for us.

Language and Life

Decision-making – Developing a Neighborhood

A 9.05 **Read the article and answer the questions below.**

Neighborhoods are changing all the time. That means someone has to make decisions about these changes. It might be urban planners or members of local government. They often have to decide between different plans for a neighborhood. They may have to think about costs, housing, and the needs of local people. How do they make their decisions?

One tool to help planners make a decision is a decision matrix. In a decision matrix, they list the important results they want for the neighborhood. For example, local people may want more houses, less traffic, or more parks. Planners develop several plans to get these results. They then score each plan against each result: −2 for a very negative effect, −1 for a negative effect, 0 for no effect, +1 for a positive effect, and +2 for a very positive effect. The plan with the highest total score is the one to choose.

People can use a decision matrix to help with all kinds of decisions, from large business decisions to personal decisions like making a budget or planning a vacation.

	Plan A	*Plan B*	*Plan C*
Result 1			
Result 2			
Result 3			
Total			

1 Who makes decisions about how neighborhoods develop? ______

2 What is the purpose of a decision matrix? ______

B IN GROUPS **Think about people in a neighborhood you know. Look at the ideas below and add your own. Which do you think are most important to them? Choose four.**

- ☐ cheaper places to live
- ☐ more public transportation
- ☐ more stores
- ☐ ______
- ☐ more job opportunities
- ☐ more green spaces
- ☐ better quality housing
- ☐ ______

C Write your four choices from **B** in the first column of the decision matrix in **E**.

D **IN PAIRS** Read the plans for neighborhood development and discuss which one you prefer.

Plan A

The city is going to build a number of apartment buildings. Half the apartments will be available to buy and half will be available to rent. The apartments will be different sizes. The first floor of each apartment building will be for stores.

Plan B

The city is going to knock down some houses and build a park. They will clean up the area, and the park will have a playground and a picnic area. There will also be basketball courts and other sports facilities.

Plan C

The city is going to build a large mall. There will be a small number of apartments for rent in the mall. The mall will include large and small stores, together with restaurants and a movie theater. A new bus route will connect downtown with the mall.

E **IN PAIRS** Score each plan from **D** from –2 to +2 for each result.

What our city needs	Plan A	Plan B	Plan C
Total			

F **IN PAIRS** Add up the total score for each plan and write it in the table in **E**. Your preferred plan is the one with the highest score. Complete the list.

First choice: Plan ____
Second choice: Plan ____
Third choice: Plan ____

MAKE IT DIGITAL

Search online for "plans for development" in your city or a city near you.

G **IN GROUPS** Compare your results from **F** and explain your thinking.

H Discuss the questions.

1 How useful was the decision matrix?
2 In what other situations do you think the decision matrix would help?

VOCABULARY review

SCORE: / 10

A Complete the text with the words from the box.

air conditioner	balcony	hall	solar panels	studio apartment
apartment hunting	couch	roommate	stove	washing machine

This month, I have to go **1** ______________ to find a new place to live. I want an apartment with built-in appliances: a **2** ______________ to wash my clothes, a **3** ______________ to cook on, and an **4** ______________ to keep the air cool. I want **5** ______________ to get energy from the sun. I'd like to have a small **6** ______________ inside the front door, and a **7** ______________ to sit outside. I don't need much furniture because right now I have a small **8** ______________ . I have a nice **9** ______________ that becomes a bed. I have a small desk and two chairs, and that's it. I'd like to get a bigger apartment, but then I'd need to find a **10** ______________ to share the bills.

GRAMMAR review

SCORE: / 10

A Choose the correct option. If both answers are correct, choose both.

1. Do you think your neighborhood **is getting** / **will get** better in the future?
2. Tomorrow morning, I **am going** / **go** apartment hunting with a friend.
3. Where **do you live** / **are you going to live** when you graduate?
4. I think I **will rent** / **am renting** an apartment downtown when I get a job.
5. Our new housemate **is arriving** / **arrives** tomorrow from his hometown.

B Complete the sentences with the correct expression of future possibility or certainty.

1. I want a studio apartment, but I ______________ have enough money for one.
2. I ______________ go back and live with my parents for a few months. I haven't decided.
3. If I don't find a job, I definitely ______________ be able to afford my own place.
4. I guess I ______________ live in another country one day. Who knows?
5. My friends and I are sure we ______________ rent a house together.

16–20 correct: You can talk about living situations and appliances. You can talk about future possibilities and certainty.
0–15 correct: Look again at the Vocabulary and Grammar sections in the unit.

TOTAL SCORE: / 20

WHAT DO YOU KNOW NOW? Look back at page 87 and add the words you know now to the boxes.

STUDY SKILLS PROBLEM SOLVING

A Take the quiz. Then go to **Study Skills** on page 135. Find the answers and learn more about problem solving.

1 Why is problem solving a useful skill to develop? Choose all the answers that apply.

a It can help you to improve your research skills.
b It can activate your knowledge on a subject.
c It helps you to develop your creativity.

2 Choose all the ways that a team can solve a problem.

a Brainstorm ideas to get different ways of looking at the problem.
b The leader of the project should make all the decisions so the team can work well.
c Research similar problems and solutions.

UNIT 10

Wellbeing

WHAT DO YOU ALREADY KNOW?

1 Think about words that describe your health.

2 IN PAIRS Share and compare your ideas. Add more words to your list.

Food

Exercise

DISCUSS & SHARE

VIDEO

3 IN GROUPS Watch the video and answer the question.

SYM Which is more important for good health, nutrition or exercise?

In this unit, you will ...

- talk about brain power, accidents, and illnesses, and improving fitness.
- use thinking skills: brainstorm, evaluate, and understand.
- read about brain power.
- use strategies to start and keep talking by agreeing and disagreeing, asking about an illness, and making a statement stronger.
- use critical thinking skills to develop an ad campaign to improve public health.
- follow a family physician to learn about this job and the skills needed for the health care industry.

LESSON 1 Power Up Your Brain!

READING

A As a class, say if each statement is true for you. Explain why or why not.

1 I generally eat well.

2 I generally get enough sleep.

B READING SKILL—Scan Read the article quickly and check (✓) the ideas it mentions.

- ☐ healthy food
- ☐ learning an instrument
- ☐ making decisions
- ☐ doing well in school
- ☐ taking a break

3 WAYS to POWER UP YOUR BRAIN!

How can you help your brain work better? Here is some advice from the experts.

• Get healthy

One way to help your **brain** is to get healthy by exercising more and eating better. In one study, people had a better **memory** after six weeks of physical training. Some studies found that if you exercise for 10 minutes before thinking about a problem, it improves your problem-solving and decision-making skills. Your **diet** is also important. Vitamins and minerals from food—like fish, vegetables, and **nuts**—help keep your brain healthy.

• Sleep better

Sleep isn't just rest for the body. It also rests your brain. During sleep, your brain organizes your **experiences**, often through dreams. When you are learning new skills, you actually get better at them while you sleep! Sleep helps you think clearly while you're awake. Most people who sleep only four to six hours in one night don't think clearly the next day.

• Keep learning

Your brain can change, something known as neuroplasticity. If you challenge your brain, it will develop more connections between its **neurons**. One thing you can do to challenge your brain is to learn a new skill, such as a new language or a musical instrument. Some people enjoy brain training—online sites and apps that use **puzzles** or other tasks to exercise your brain. Many of these sites and apps don't have much effect on the brain, and they certainly won't make you more **intelligent**. However, psychologists have created some types of puzzles that make your brain work faster. Doing these tasks makes some people feel sharper in their everyday lives.

C 10.01 Read the article in B again and answer the questions.

1 How might you improve your decision-making skills? ______

2 What happens to most people after only getting four to six hours sleep? ______

3 Does brain training work? ______

D THINKING SKILL—Brainstorm What are other ways you could develop your brain?

VOCABULARY

A Complete each sentence with a bold word from the text in READING B.

1 Your ______ is all the things you usually eat.

2 Your ______ are the things that happen to you each day.

3 ______ are games or tasks where you have to think carefully to find the answer.

4 ______ are the cells in your brain.

5 If you are ______, you are smart and you think very clearly about things.

6 Your ______ is the organ inside your head that controls your body.

7 Your ______ is the part of you that remembers things.

8 ______ are the dry fruit of some trees. They have a hard shell.

GRAMMAR zero and first conditional

A Read the sentences. Then choose the correct answer.

Zero conditional

If someone sleeps more, his or her brain works better.
if clause — result clause

First conditional

If you start learning a new skill, your brain will work faster.
if clause — result clause

1 The zero conditional expresses general facts and scientific truths / real possibilities in the present or future.
2 The first conditional expresses general facts and scientific truths / real possibilities in the present or future.

For more practice, go to page 156.

B Circle the verbs in each clause of the sentences in A. Then complete the grammar rules.

Zero conditional

1 In the *if* clause, use the ____________ tense.
2 In the result clause, use the ____________ tense.

First conditional

3 In the *if* clause, use the ____________ tense.
4 In the result clause, use ____________ + base form of the verb.

C Complete the text with the correct form of words from the box.

be get learn do grow practice

If you **1** ____________ a new skill, your brain **2** ____________. The density of white matter in your brain increases and your neurons work better. However, it has to be an active skill, such as learning the piano. You **3** ____________ better if you **4** ____________ every day. Each time you practice, you create new connections between your neurons. Play for just a short time and it makes a difference. If you **5** ____________ that for a year, you **6** ____________ amazed at your progress.

D IN PAIRS Discuss if you agree or disagree with the statements. Explain your answers.

1 You can do anything if you try hard enough.
2 If you relax and stop worrying, you will succeed.

SPEAKING

A Choose the option that you agree with the most.

1 If I study ..., I learn more.
 a alone b with friends

2 I will do better on an exam if I ... the night before.
 a relax b study for hours

B IN PAIRS Compare your answers from A and discuss the reasons for your choices. Explain why you don't agree with the other choices. Use the Confident Communicator box to help you.

CONFIDENT COMMUNICATOR
START TALKING

Use the following expressions to say you agree or disagree with an idea.
I agree that it's a good idea to study with other people.
I disagree that it's easier to concentrate if you listen to music

Accidents and Illnesses

VOCABULARY accidents and illnesses

A Complete the phrases with the words from the box.

ankle head throat arm leg

1
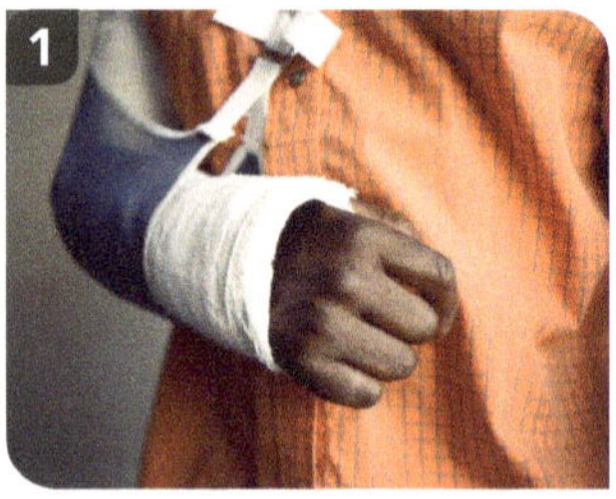
break your / have a broken ________

2

have a ________ache

3
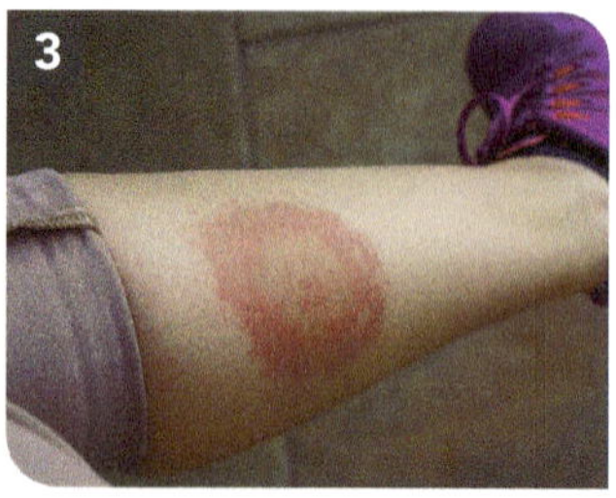
have a rash on your ________

4

sprain your / have a sprained ________

5
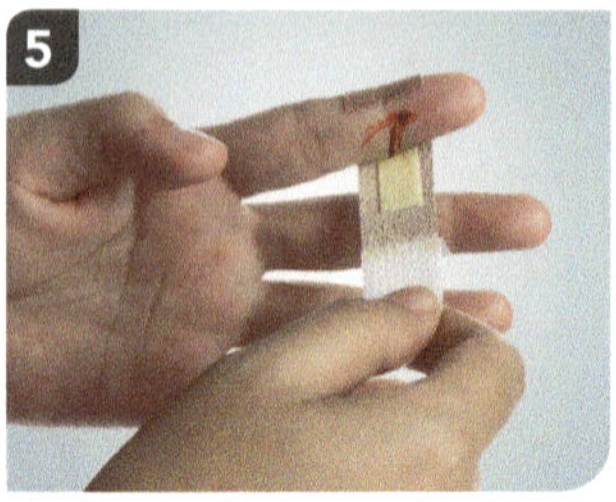
have a cut

6
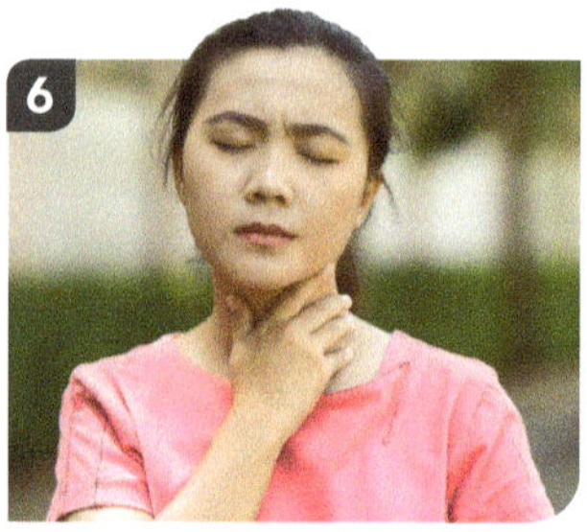
have a sore ________

7

have a cold

8
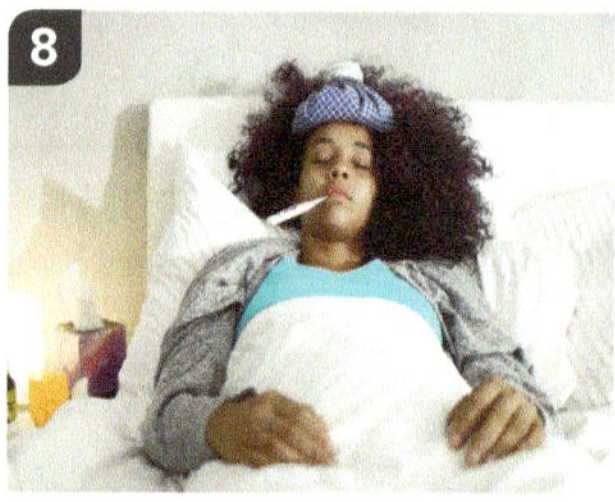
have a fever

B IN PAIRS Discuss the questions.

1 Have you ever hurt a part of your body? What happened?
2 When was the last time you felt sick?

MAKE IT YOURS

Make a list of other words you might need to talk about accidents and illnesses.

GRAMMAR second conditional

A Read the table and choose the correct option to complete the grammar rule.

Second conditional

If you broke your arm, it would / might / could be hard to drive.
if clause — result clause

1 We use the second conditional to talk about …
  a real possibilities in the present or future.
  b hypothetical or impossible situations in the present or future.

For more practice, go to page 157.

B Read the sentence. Then complete the grammar rules.

If I **broke** a bone, I **would** go to the hospital.

1 In the *if* clause, use the ________ tense.
2 In the result clause, use ________ + base form.

MAKE IT REAL

Note that in formal English we use *if* + *I/he/she/it* + ***were*** instead of *was*. However, many English speakers do not use this form anymore and simply use *was*.

C IN PAIRS **Discuss the questions.**

What would you do if you …

1 lost your phone? 2 won the lottery? 3 broke your leg?

LISTENING

A 10.02 **Listen to the podcast and choose *True* or *False*.**

1	Madison Gray is a doctor.	True / False
2	The right skills are very important.	True / False
3	You should help someone up right away if he or she falls.	True / False
4	You should always call an ambulance after a fall.	True / False
5	With a broken arm, you should first find something long and hard.	True / False

B 10.02 LISTENING SKILL—Listen for cause and effect **Listen again and answer the questions.**

1 If someone was injured, and you helped the person up, what could happen?

____

2 If someone breaks an arm, why do you have to stop any bleeding first?

____

C IN GROUPS THINKING SKILL—Evaluate **Should we teach first aid in schools? Why or why not? Discuss.**

PRONUNCIATION intonation in conditional sentences

A 10.03 **Choose the correct intonation. Then listen and check.**

1 If I had a cough, ↗ I would buy some medicine. ↘

2 If I had a cough, ↘ I would buy some medicine. ↗

B 10.04 **Practice saying the sentences with the correct intonation.**

1 If I broke my leg, I would call an ambulance.
2 If I had a rash, I'd search for information online.
3 If I sprained my ankle, I'd ask a friend for help.

SPEAKING

A IN PAIRS **Read the situation and discuss your answers. Use the Confident Communicator box to help you.**

A friend who only speaks English is visiting you. How would you help your friend in each of the situations? What would you do if he or she …

- had a headache?
- had a cough and a sore throat?
- had a fever?
- had a sprained ankle?

B IN PAIRS **Role-play the situation in A. Student A, you are the English-speaking friend. Describe your problem. Student B, try to help Student A.**

CONFIDENT COMMUNICATOR
KEEP TALKING

Use the following phrases to ask for and give details about someone who is sick.

What's wrong? *What's the matter?*
Where does it hurt? *Where do you feel pain?*
I have a fever, and my head hurts.
It's not just my head. It's also my throat.

LESSON 3 Improve Your Fitness

VOCABULARY collocations with *get*

A Complete the sentences (1–8) with *get* and a word from the box.

home | in shape | sick | tired | hungry | ready | started | upset

1 I joined a gym because I want to ___get in shape.___
2 I usually just turn the TV on when I ______________ from work.
3 I don't seem to have much energy, and I ______________ easily.
4 My brother is training to ______________ for the marathon next month.
5 There's a lot of work to do, so let's ______________!
6 Don't ______________. I'm sure everything will be okay.
7 I always ______________ by 10 a.m. because I don't eat breakfast.
8 When you are in bad shape, you often ______________ and take time off work.

B IN PAIRS Discuss the questions.

1 What do you usually do when you get home from class/work?
2 What are some ways people can get in shape?
3 Do you eat only at mealtimes, or do you get hungry between meals?

LISTENING

A Mark the scale with how active you are. Compare with a partner and explain.

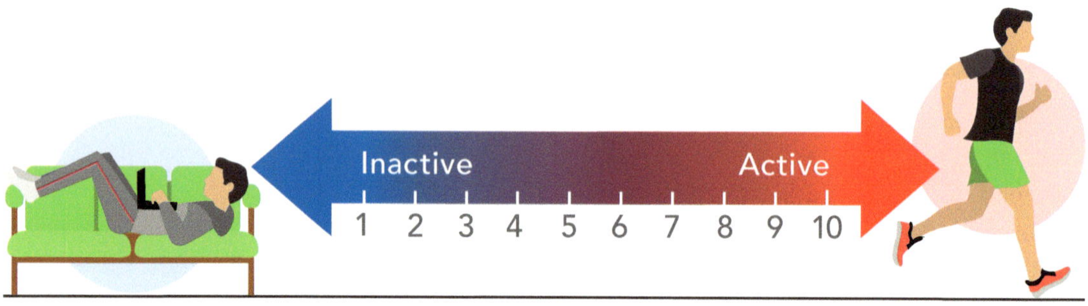

B 10.05 LISTENING SKILL—Listen for gist Check (✓) the ideas that are mentioned.

☐ This program is for people who run a lot.
☐ You need to eat well to get in shape.
☐ With Couch to 5K, you start slowly and then get faster.

C 10.05 Listen again and complete the sentences with a word or short phrase.

1 You might need to see ______________ if you have health problems.
2 In Week 1, you run for ______________.
3 You'll run for 30 minutes after ______________.
4 When you eat the right things, you don't ______________ when you're exercising.

D IN PAIRS THINKING SKILL—Understand Discuss the questions.

1 Do programs like Couch to 5K work for everyone? Why or why not?
2 Is it important to be in shape? In what ways?

WRITING

A **Read the comment from a website. In your own words, explain how Hugo got in shape.**

A small change can make a big difference! I wanted to get in shape, but I didn't have time to go to the gym. I drove to college every day, so I didn't get much exercise. One day, I decided to park my car far away from the building I needed to go to on campus, and I walked the rest of the way. Each week, I parked a little farther away. After a month, I started to feel better. After two months, people started to ask me if I was working out! There are always ways to get more exercise into your life. Why don't you try walking a little more? Start small and you'll be amazed at what you can do!

Hugo Oliveira, Curitiba, Brazil • 1 day ago

B IN PAIRS **Choose three small life changes you would like to try. Discuss why you would like to try them.**

- ☐ eat smaller meals
- ☐ use a fitness app
- ☐ eat at the dining table
- ☐ eat a protein-rich breakfast
- ☐ use a calorie-counting app
- ☐ stop keeping snacks at home
- ☐ drink more water
- ☐ walk instead of drive
- ☐ walk during breaks from work/class

C **Complete the sentences to persuade someone to make a change.**

1 You should ____________________.
2 Why don't you ____________________?
3 Have you thought about ____________________?
4 I suggest ____________________.

D **Imagine you made one of the small life changes in B. What happened? Write a comment for a fitness website about your experience.**

SPEAKING

A **Check (✓) the problems that keep you from getting completely in shape and healthy. Then add your own ideas.**

- ☐ not enough money
- ☐ not interested
- ☐ can't cook
- ☐ no gyms near me
- ☐ don't like sports
- ☐ don't know about healthy eating

____________________ ____________________

B **For each problem you checked in A, imagine what you would do if that problem didn't exist. Make notes in your notebook.**

There are no gyms near me. If there were a gym near me, I would join and start exercising.

C IN PAIRS **Discuss the problems from A and what you would do if they didn't exist. Use the Confident Communicator box to help you.**

CONFIDENT COMMUNICATOR
START TALKING

Use *really* to make a statement stronger.
I was ***really*** *out of shape, so I started playing tennis.*
It was a ***really*** *small change, but it helped a lot.*

Language and Life

Critical Thinking – Improving Public Health

A 10.06 **Read the article and choose the correct option.**

Many countries face serious public health problems. One example is obesity. According to the Organisation for Economic Co-operation and Development, one in two adults and nearly one in six children in its member countries are overweight or obese. That puts pressure on health services. Some countries are looking at ways of improving public health.

One way is to encourage people to eat better. Some countries, such as the United States and the United Kingdom, have five-a-day campaigns. They tell people that they should eat five portions of fruit or vegetables each day. Many countries have laws about labels on food. Producers have to show the amount of fat, protein, and carbohydrates in each food. Some countries have a "traffic light" system. Green means the food has a small amount of fat, sugar, and salt. Yellow means the food has a medium amount. Red means there's a high amount of fat, sugar, or salt. The labels help people make better choices.

Public health departments are always looking for new ideas to improve public health.

1 About ____________ of all adults are overweight or obese in OECD countries.
   a a third b a sixth c half
2 Obesity causes problems for ____________.
   a all countries b health services c mainly children
3 Some countries say you should eat ____________ each day.
   a no more than five meals b five types of vegetable c five servings of fruit and vegetables
4 In a "traffic light" system, you can eat less fat if you choose a label where the fat is in ____________.
   a green b yellow c red

B Check the brainstorming tips you have used.

- ☐ Suggest as many ideas as you can.
- ☐ Accept all ideas, useful and not useful, and write them down.
- ☐ Make sure everyone in your group offers an idea.
- ☐ Go online and quickly look at other people's ideas.
- ☐ Try to put ideas together and see what happens.
- ☐ Look at a problem from different points of view.

C IN GROUPS Brainstorm ways you could help the public health department improve the health of each of the people. Make notes of all your ideas.

a child

a young adult

a senior citizen

1 **Child:** *ban cartoon characters from unhealthy food packaging*

2 **Young adult:** *create a cool fitness app*

3 **Senior citizen:** *provide low-cost, simple, healthy recipes*

D IN GROUPS Choose one age group. Look at your ideas. Cross out ideas you think wouldn't work. Explain why.

If we banned cartoon characters from unhealthy food packaging, children would still want that kind of food.

E IN GROUPS Choose your best ideas. Explain why those ideas would work.

Idea 1: ______

Idea 2: ______

Idea 3: ______

F IN GROUPS Present your ideas to the class. Predict what would happen if the public health department used your idea.

If we created a cool fitness app for young adults, they would want to get more exercise.

G Discuss the questions.

1 Why is it important to consider different points of view?
2 In what other situations do you need to think critically and creatively?

MAKE IT DIGITAL

Research ways public health officials in your country are working to solve your country's most serious health problems.

VOCABULARY review

SCORE: / 10

A Complete the sentences. The first letter of the missing words is given.

Ella: Oh, Frank! You have a **1** b__________ arm! How did you do that?
Frank: I was trying to get **2** i__________ s__________ and I changed my **3** d__________ so that I was eating better.
Ella: Oh, yes. I remember.
Frank: Well, it wasn't working well, so I decided to try skateboarding. I'm a beginner, but I tried to do a few tricks. That wasn't very **4** i__________. In fact, it was kind of stupid. It was going OK, but then I got **5** t__________ and made a mistake. I fell on my arm! I had to go to the hospital.
Ella: That's awful!
Frank: The next day, after I got **6** h__________ from the hospital, I got **7** s__________. I had a temperature of 100 degrees, and I had a **8** s__________ throat. I had a **9** f__________!
Ella: Oh, no! I hope you didn't get **10** u__________!
Frank: Nah. It was fine. But I'm looking forward to getting back on my skateboard!

GRAMMAR review

SCORE: / 10

A Match the sentence beginnings (1–5) to the sentence endings (a–e). Write the letter.

1 If you eat better, ____
2 If you buy less candy, ____
3 You probably exercise more ____
4 It's possible to run 5K ____
5 If you don't have a personal trainer, ____

a if you live close to a gym.
b you will have more energy.
c you might not do the exercises correctly.
d if you run a little farther each week.
e you won't have so many problems with your teeth!

B Complete the sentences with verbs in the correct tense. Add any other words you need.

1 What __________ (you/cook) if you wanted to help your family lose weight?
2 I __________ (go) to the gym more often if I had more time.
3 If people __________ (eat) five portions of fruit and vegetables a day, there would be less obesity.
4 You'd get more exercise if you __________ (walk) to class instead of driving.
5 If I __________ (have) more money, I would probably join a gym.

16–20 correct: You can use collocations with *get* and talk about accidents and illnesses.
You can recognize zero, first, and second conditionals.
0–15 correct: Look again at the Vocabulary and Grammar sections in the unit.

TOTAL SCORE: / 20

WHAT DO YOU KNOW NOW? Look back at page 97 and add the words you know now to the boxes.

FOLLOW A PRO HEALTH CARE

Take the quiz about the medical profession. Then go to **Follow A Pro** on page 136. Find the answers and learn more about the health care industry.

1 How many doctors are there in the US?
a about 250,000 **b** about 500,000 **c** over 1 million

2 Patients with female surgeons do better than those with male surgeons.
a True **b** False

3 Where was the first hospital in North America built?
a Toronto **b** New York **c** Mexico City

UNIT 11

Use and Reuse

WHAT DO YOU ALREADY KNOW?

1 **Think of words you know about recycling and improving the environment. Write the words.**

2 **IN PAIRS** **Share and compare your information. Add more words to your lists.**

Save the Earth

VIDEO

DISCUSS & SHARE

3 **IN GROUPS** **Watch the video and answer the question.**

SYM Which do you use, paper or plastic?

In this unit, you will ...

- talk about what things are made of, how new materials are made, and how plastic can be recycled.
- use thinking skills: brainstorm, understand, and analyze.
- read about how T-shirts are made and recycled.
- use strategies to start and keep talking by ordering steps in a process, stating who made something, and suggesting alternatives.
- use innovation skills to brainstorm ways to upcycle materials.
- learn tips about using precise language in academic writing.

READING

A **As a class, discuss how you think people make the following items: jeans, shoes, jewelry.**

B 11.01 **Read the article and choose the correct options.**

From Seed to T-shirt

T-shirts are a basic part of almost everyone's closet. Over two billion T-shirts are sold every year around the world. So how are they made? And where do they **end up**?

The story starts with the seed of the cotton plant. The plants are grown on large farms. The cotton is collected and sent to a factory. There, it is cleaned and made into **yarn**. The yarn is made into cloth. This is used to make T-shirts.

The T-shirts are then **transported** around the world. Just take a look at the label on one of your T-shirts and see how far it came! The T-shirts go into stores and are sold to consumers. That's you. You probably have the T-shirt for a while, and it is worn, washed, and dried again and again. When you decide to **get rid of** it, you have a few options. You might throw it in the trash. But if you knew how much of the Earth's **natural resources** go into making a T-shirt, you might think again! A lot of energy and water are used in making and washing clothes. A lot of chemicals are used in this process, too.

One option is to recycle your old T-shirts. When a T-shirt is sent to a recycling center, it is made into other things, such as cleaning cloths. Another idea is to upcycle your T-shirts. Old T-shirts are sometimes made into belts, scarves, or bags.

1 Where does the story of a T-shirt start?
  a in a factory **b** on a farm

2 What information on a T-shirt label does the writer mention?
  a the country the T-shirt comes from **b** how to wash the T-shirt

3 Where in the lifecycle do we use a lot of energy and water?
  a growing the cotton plant **b** producing and cleaning the T-shirt

4 When a T-shirt is upcycled, it might become …
  a a scarf. **b** another T-shirt.

C READING SKILL—Understand words from context **Find the words from the box in the text in B. Read the context and explain what you think they mean.**

consumers label upcycle

D THINKING SKILL—Brainstorm **What other uses for old T-shirts can you think of? Make a list in your notebook.**

VOCABULARY

A **Match the bold words from the text in READING B to the definitions (1–5).**

1 very long, thin piece of cotton or wool: ____________

2 moved from one place to another by truck, train, or boat: ____________

3 come to a final place or situation that is not expected: ____________

4 things we use from the Earth, such as water, oil, or trees: ____________

5 throw away: ____________

GRAMMAR simple present passive

A Underline examples of the passive voice in the article in READING B.

Over two billion T-shirts are sold every year around the world.

B Choose the correct option to complete the rules for forming and using the present passive voice.

1. Use the auxiliary *be* / *have* in the simple present followed by the simple past / past participle of the verb.
2. Use the present passive to focus on the thing that does / receives the action.
3. Use the present passive when we don't know / are interested in who or what does something.
4. Use the present passive when it's important / obvious or unimportant who or what does something.

For more practice, go to page 157.

C Complete the sentences with the present passive form of the verb in parentheses.

Do you know how a notebook **1** ______________ (make)? First of all, trees **2** ______________ (cut) down. The wood from the trees **3** ______________ (turn) into paper. Color **4** ______________ (remove) from the paper to make it white. Lines **5** ______________ (print) on the paper. Glue **6** ______________ (used) to stick the pages together. Finally, a cover **7** ______________ (put) on the notebook.

D IN PAIRS Look at what you are wearing and what you have with you. Discuss what your things are made of.

A: I'm wearing a T-shirt. It's made of cotton.

B: I have a bag. It's made of plastic and metal.

SPEAKING

A Use the prompts to write sentences in the simple present passive.

1. water / drink by the consumer ______________
2. plastic / melt to make a bottle ______________
3. oil / take from the ground ______________
4. bottle / transport to a store ______________
5. oil / make into plastic ______________
6. the bottle / recycle ______________
7. the bottle / send to landfill ______________
8. the bottle / fill with water ______________

B IN PAIRS Look at the pictures and tell your partner about the lifecycle of a plastic bottle. Use the Confident Communicator box to help you.

First, oil is taken from the ground. Then, …

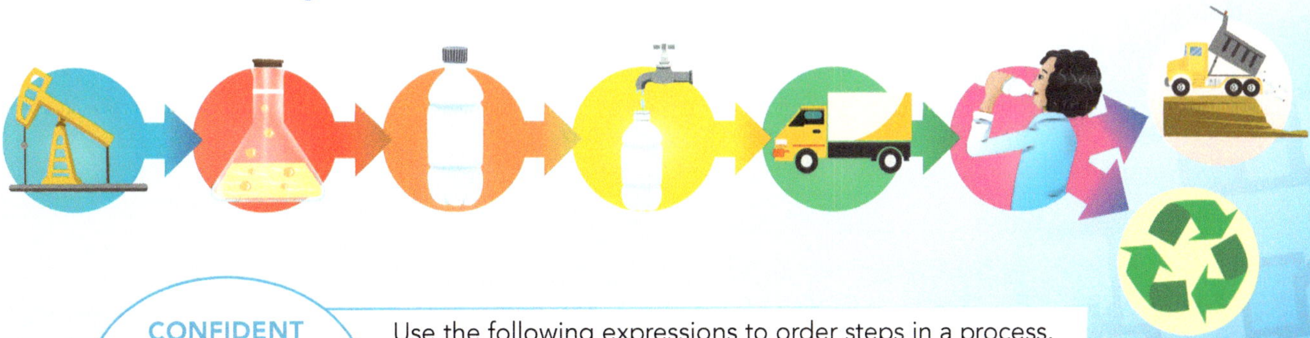

CONFIDENT COMMUNICATOR
START TALKING

Use the following expressions to order steps in a process.

First, it's grown …
Then, it's transported …
After that, it's made into …
Next, it's painted …
Finally, it's sold …

LESSON 2 An Accidental Discovery

VOCABULARY clothing materials

A IN PAIRS Discuss the questions.

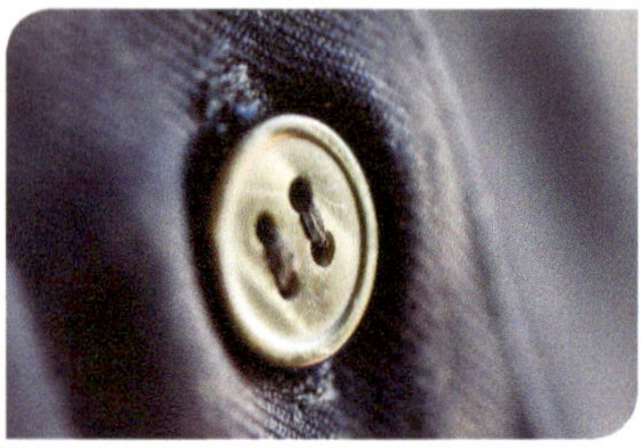

button

zipper

Velcro

fur

fake fur

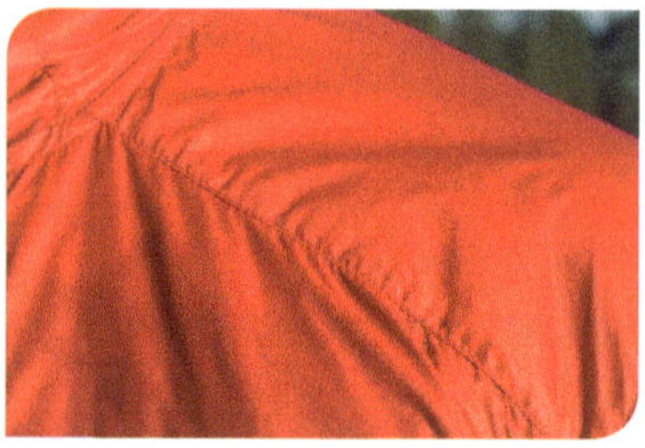

nylon

1 Do you prefer buttons, zippers, or Velcro on your clothes? Why?
2 Can you tell the difference between real and fake fur?
3 What do you think of clothes made from fur? Do you think people should wear them?
4 Do you prefer clothes made from nylon or clothes made from natural materials, such as cotton or silk? Why?

B IN PAIRS Describe how your clothes and items fasten and unfasten.

PRONUNCIATION silent *t*

A 11.02 Listen to the words. Notice that the *t* is silent.

castle whistle wrestle fasten listen soften

B 11.03 Listen to the sentences and practice saying them.

1 Listen to the way he whistles.
2 You fasten and unfasten the jacket with a zipper.
3 Chemicals are used to soften the cloth.

LISTENING

A 11.04 LISTENING SKILL—Listen for key words Listen to an interview. Complete the sentences with the words or phrases you hear.

1 Angela says Velcro ____________ with the help of a dog.
2 Plants stuck to the ____________ of George de Mestral's dog.
3 In the beginning, Velcro was made of ____________.
4 It became ____________ when it was used by astronauts.
5 In the 1980s, Velcro was used on ____________ sneakers.

B 11.04 **Listen again and choose *True* or *False*.**

1 George de Mestral was looking for plants while he was walking his dog. True / False
2 The burrs had hooks that caught onto his pants. True / False
3 De Mestral soon produced a commercial product. True / False
4 In the beginning, Velcro was used on clothes and bags. True / False
5 Velcro was used on sneakers in the 1970s. True / False

C IN PAIRS THINKING SKILL—Understand **Explain why NASA used Velcro in the 1960s.**

GRAMMAR simple past passive

A **Read the sentences. Choose the correct option to complete the grammar rules.**

De Mestral noticed that his dog **was covered** in burrs. His pants **were** also **covered** in them.

1 We form the simple past passive with the verb ***be*** / ***have*** in the simple past followed by the **past participle** / *–ing form* of the verb.
2 We use the simple past passive when we are talking about the past and …
- we want to focus on the thing that **does** / **receives** the action.
- we **are interested in** / **don't know** who or what does something.
- it's **unimportant** / **essential** who or what does something.

For more practice, go to page 158.

MAKE IT DIGITAL

Search online for the history of an invention (cell phone, TV, the internet, etc.). Find out how it was invented. Tell the class.

B **Complete the text with the simple past passive form of the verbs in parentheses.**

Superglue **1** _____________ (discover) by accident. In 1942, Dr. Harry Coover was trying to make clear plastic. This **2** _____________ (need) for military equipment. A number of chemicals **3** _____________ (create) in the laboratory, and one of them was called cyanoacrylate. It wasn't a clear plastic, but it was a strong glue. It **4** _____________ (develop) because it wasn't useful for that project. Nine years later, Coover was working on jet planes and cyanoacrylate **5** _____________ (use) again. This time, Coover realized how useful it was. Superglue **6** _____________ (release) as a commercial product in 1958.

SPEAKING

A **Answer the questions for you.**

1 Think of something that was bought for, made for, or given to you. What was it? _____________
2 When was it bought/made/given? _____________
3 Who was it bought/made/given by? _____________
4 How did you feel when it was bought/made/given? _____________

B IN PAIRS **Discuss your object from A. Ask and answer questions about it. Use the Confident Communicator box to help you.**

A: I have a guitar. It was bought for me by my grandfather.
B: When was it bought for you?
A: A year ago. It was given to me for my birthday, and …

CONFIDENT COMMUNICATOR
KEEP TALKING

Use *by* to say who or what did something in the passive.
It was made by my uncle.

LESSON 3 Using and Reusing Plastic

LISTENING

A You are going to listen to a lecture. Look at the picture. What do you think the lecture will be about?

B 11.05 LISTENING SKILL—Listen for gist Listen to the first part of the lecture and choose the correct summary.

1 Thato faces a number of problems. She works in a school that has no electricity. The children are tired after their trip to school. They find it hard to do their schoolwork.

2 Thato thought about the problems of schoolchildren. Getting to and from school is sometimes dangerous. They live without electricity and it is difficult for them to do their homework.

C 11.06 Listen to the rest of the lecture. Then complete the sentences with the words from the box.

a light	drivers	plastic bags	schoolbags

1 There is a problem with _____________ in South Africa.
2 Thato made _____________ out of trash.
3 Her products have a solar panel, a battery, and _____________.
4 The children can be seen by _____________.

D THINKING SKILL—Analyze Categorize the materials from the box.

aluminum	ceramic	cotton	leather	plastic	steel
cardboard	copper	glass	nylon	rubber	

1 can be recycled easily: _____________
2 can't be recycled easily: _____________

VOCABULARY collocations connected to materials

A Match the phrases (1–4) to the definitions (a–d). Write the letter.

1 cause pollution _____
2 harm wildlife _____
3 last a long time _____
4 reduce the amount we use _____

a stay in the environment for years
b have a bad effect on animals
c use less
d have a bad effect on the environment

B IN PAIRS Discuss the questions.

1 What materials cause pollution where you live?
2 Does the pollution in your area harm wildlife?
3 What materials last a long time in the environment?
4 Do you think people should reduce the amount of plastic they use?

MAKE IT YOURS

Are there any materials around you that you don't know the English word for? Look online or in a dictionary and find out.

WRITING

A Read the email and answer the questions.

New Message

To: supporter@mail.co Cc Bcc

Subject: Spread the Word

Dear Supporter,
Thank you for supporting Use Less Plastic. We rely on people like you to get the message out that we need to reduce the amount we use. Plastic lasts in the environment for thousands of years and harms wildlife. We're writing to you now to ask for your help. We want you to send an email to your local news website to explain why we need to Use Less Plastic. Explain that plastic causes pollution. And remember to tell them what we can all do to Use Less Plastic.
We need to educate people about this problem to solve it.
Sincerely,
The Use Less Plastic Team

Send

1 Who does the Use Less Plastic team want you to write to? ______
2 What three things do they want you to mention? ______

B Choose the correct option.

1 The … for this is that we use too much plastic.
a result b reason c fact
2 This is … we use too much plastic.
a since b result c because
3 We are responsible for this problem … we use too much plastic.
a since b reason c why

C IN PAIRS Complete the notes.

1 Main causes of plastic pollution: plastic bags, ______
2 Problems it causes: trash in the streets, ______
3 How to use less plastic: reuse plastic bags, ______

D In your notebook, write an email to your local news website to explain why people need to use less plastic.

SPEAKING

A Think about your own use of plastic. Answer for you.

1 How many of these things do you buy or use each week?
drinks in plastic bottles: ______ drinking straws: ______
drinks in to-go cups: ______ (other) ______ : ______
items in plastic packaging: ______
2 Add up your weekly score and multiply it by 52. Write your annual total plastic items here: ______

B IN PAIRS Compare your scores and discuss how you could use less plastic. Use the Confident Communicator box to help you.

CONFIDENT COMMUNICATOR
START TALKING

Use *One / Another option is* + *to* infinitive to suggest alternatives.
One option is to use a refillable drinking bottle.
Another option is to take your own bags to the store.

Language and Life

Innovation – Upcycling Projects

A 11.07 **Read the article and list the examples of upcycling that are mentioned.**

plant containers made from old rubber boots

upcycled art by Tim Noble and Sue Webster

UPCYCLING PROJECTS

We humans use a lot of materials. Take plastic, for example.

According to Statista, every year, around 350 million metric tons of plastic are produced around the world. Sadly, not much of it is recycled. In fact, about half of the plastic is used just once and is then sent to a landfill, according to Plastic Oceans International. In 2007, Charles Fishman of *Fast Company Magazine* reported that a million plastic bottles are bought every minute of every day in the US, but only around 23% are recycled. Four trillion plastic bags are produced each year, and only 1% are recycled, according to Waste Management. Our use of other plastics is not much better. Plastic use is a big problem.

Many people are looking at ways to upcycle different materials. Upcycling involves finding new uses for materials at the end of their original use. In one project, a greenhouse was created using old plastic water bottles. In others, large coffee cans or old rubber boots were turned into containers for plants, and old rubber tires became notebook covers. Artists, too, upcycle materials. Tim Noble and Sue Webster, two British artists, create what look like piles of trash. When a light shines on the trash from a certain angle, it makes an interesting shadow on the wall.

These days institutions such as colleges and companies are looking for smarter ways to use materials. This involves reducing the amount of materials they use and thinking of ways to upcycle materials so that they last a long time.

B IN GROUPS **Read the situation and discuss the questions.**

Your college supports a local upcycling campaign. They want to encourage people to upcycle more. They want students to suggest interesting ways to upcycle. Here are the main problems the college wants to solve:

1 Students use a lot of plastic water bottles. They create trash and many of them go to the landfill. Are there ways they could be upcycled?

2 The college receives a lot of deliveries every day, which means there are a lot of cardboard boxes. They are usually recycled, but that uses energy. Are there ways they could be upcycled?

C Write about plastic and cardboard waste at your school or workplace.

1 Estimate how many plastic bottles are thrown out every day.

____

2 Estimate how much cardboard is thrown away each week.

____

D Brainstorm ways of upcycling. Write as many ideas as you can.

1 Ideas for plastic bottle reuse and upcycling

use plastic bottles as plant containers

____

____

2 Ideas for cardboard reuse and upcycling

use boxes to store books

____

____

E Choose your best two ideas from D and add more detail. How will your idea work? Who will do it?

Idea 1:

____

____

____

Idea 2:

____

____

____

F Tell the class about your ideas from E.

G What are your favorite ideas? Take a class vote.

H Discuss the questions.

1 Did working in a group help you imagine new ideas?
2 In what other situations do you need to innovate to solve problems?

MAKE IT DIGITAL

Search online to see if any of your ideas from **E** are available online, and find more ideas for ways to upcycle other products.

VOCABULARY review

SCORE: / 10

A Unscramble and write the word in parentheses.

1 Many jackets are fastened with a __________ (ppzeir).
2 We need to use fewer natural __________ (oseercus).
3 I can't __________ (snnefatu) my jacket.
4 I'm trying to __________ (deecru) the amount of plastic I use.
5 Are your socks made of __________ (lnyno)?
6 A __________ (otubnt) came off my shirt!
7 I need __________ (rayn) to make a sweater.
8 Plastic causes a lot of __________ (inltolpou).
9 Does waste harm __________ (leliiwdf) in your area?
10 The __________ (eblla) says "Made in China."

GRAMMAR review

SCORE: / 10

A Complete the sentences with the present passive form of words in the box.

add make make take wear

Sweaters **1** __________ of wool. The wool **2** __________ from sheep. It **3** __________ into yarn. Color **4** __________ to the yarn, and it is knitted into sweaters. Sweaters **5** __________ during cold weather.

B Rewrite the sentences in the passive.

1 My uncle bought this bag for me.
____
2 Did the Chinese invent paper?
____
3 Someone discovered penicillin by accident.
____
4 People first used CDs for music in 1982.
____
5 They didn't use plastic 150 years ago.
____

16–20 correct: You can use collocations with materials and describe clothing materials. You can use simple present passive and simple past passive.
0–15 correct: Look again at the Vocabulary and Grammar sections in the unit.

TOTAL SCORE: / 20

WHAT DO YOU KNOW NOW? Look back at page 107 and add the words you know now to the box.

STUDY SKILLS USING PRECISE LANGUAGE IN ACADEMIC WRITING

Take the quiz. Then go to **Study Skills** on page 137. Find the answers and learn more about using precise language in academic writing.

1 It's natural for people to enjoy spending time outdoors. This statement is …
a a fact. **b** an opinion.

2 A lot of people were killed in the earthquake. This statement is …
a precise. **b** imprecise.

3 Eighty-five percent of people in the US go to work by car. This statement is …
a precise. **b** imprecise.

4 About 150,000 people are employed by this company. This statement uses …
a the active voice. **b** the passive voice.

UNIT 12
I'm a Member

WHAT DO YOU ALREADY KNOW?

1 Think about your social life and the activities you like to do with other people. Write the words.

2 IN PAIRS Share and compare your ideas. Add more words to your lists.

Social life

VIDEO

DISCUSS & SHARE

3 IN GROUPS Watch the video and answer the question.

SYM Do you prefer to have friends who are similar to you or different from you?

In this unit, you will ...

- talk about types of communities, networking, and youth subcultures.
- use thinking skills: analyze and understand.
- read about the different types of social groups.
- use strategies to start and keep talking by making guesses, showing certainty, and adding a further point.
- use media literacy skills to design an ad campaign to reach a target group.
- follow an entrepreneur to learn about this job and the skills needed for the business field.

LESSON 1 Different Groups

READING

A **Do you belong to a club or other social group? If so, what activities do you do in this group? Discuss as a class.**

B 12.01 READING SKILL—Understand the main ideas **Read the article. Then match the sentence halves.**

TYPES of COMMUNITY

We all **belong** to different social groups. We choose some of them ourselves, and some of them are chosen for us. The social groups we belong to often give us support. They also say a lot about who we are and how we see ourselves.

There are many different types of community. One type is community of place. The place could be a neighborhood, a region, or a country. A second is community of interest. The people might all be interested in a certain hobby or a certain type of music, for example. A third is community of **purpose**. People in this type of community **share** the same purpose, such as learning a language or running a successful company. A fourth is community of practice. This is a group of people who share the same profession.

Each type of community can offer different things to its members. A community of place might offer people to **chat** with and to support you in difficult times. A community of interest can give you friendship and a way to learn more about a subject. A community of purpose can help you learn ways of achieving your goals. Also, people working together can often **achieve** more than a person working by himself or herself. A community of practice gives you opportunities to share ideas as well as the chance to **network**.

Any particular group might be more than one type of community. For example, a local cycling club is a community of place and a community of interest. If the members decided to raise money for a local charity, they would also be a community of purpose.

Read more

1 People in a community of place _____
2 People in a community of interest _____
3 People in a community of purpose _____
4 People in a community of practice _____

a want to achieve the same thing.
b might have the same hobby.
c might do the same job.
d might live in the same area.

C THINKING SKILL—Analyze **List your social groups in your notebook. Then write what type of community each of your social groups belongs to.**

VOCABULARY

A **Replace the underlined words in the sentences with synonyms from the box.**

achieve	chat	purpose of	belong to	network	share

1 You need to meet people in your profession if you want to find a better job. ____________
2 You learn more if you tell other people your ideas. ____________
3 I hope to do a lot in my career. ____________
4 I am a member of a chess club. ____________
5 The reason for our study group is to practice our English. ____________
6 I'm very busy studying, so I don't have time to sit and talk with friends. ____________

GRAMMAR reflexive pronouns

A Read the article in READING B again and complete the table.

	Subject pronouns	Reflexive pronouns
Singular	I	myself
	you	yourself
	he	**1**
	she	**2**
	it	itself
Plural	we	**3**
	you	yourselves
	they	themselves

MAKE IT REAL

Reflexive pronouns are used in many idiomatic expressions in English. Examples are *teach yourself to do something* (learn something without a teacher), *help yourself to something* (get something without the assistance of your host), and *behave yourself* (behave correctly).

B Match the functions (1–2) to the examples (a–b). Write the letter.

We use reflexive pronouns …

1 when the subject and the object of the sentence are the same. _____

2 to mean "without help from another person." _____

a *Did you start the fan club yourself or did you have help?*

b *I see myself as a professional person.*

For more practice, go to page 158.

C Complete the text with reflexive pronouns.

The way we see **1** _____________ may depend on the groups we belong to. For example, if you have a large social life, you probably consider **2** _____________ to be friendly and confident. People who belong to a sports club may think of **3** _____________ as good members of a team. This can help in their future careers. Different groups can also give you different experiences. Someone who joins a community of purpose, such as a local action group, may achieve something that he or she can't achieve by **4** _____________ or **5** _____________. If you can't find the right group, then you might think about starting one **6** _____________. This can also be an interesting experience.

PRONUNCIATION /s/ vs. /ʃ/

A 12.02 **Listen and choose the word or phrase you hear.**

1 self / shelf
2 yourself / your shelf
3 herself / her shelf
4 sock / shock
5 so / show
6 sign / shine

SPEAKING

A IN PAIRS **Discuss the questions. Use the Confident Communicator box to help you.**

1 What different communities of interest do you belong to or did you belong to in the past?
2 What do/did you enjoy the most about each different group?

CONFIDENT COMMUNICATOR
START TALKING

To talk about something when you're not completely sure or when you're still thinking about your opinion, use *I guess*:
I guess I enjoy sharing ideas with people the most.

Developing Your Network

VOCABULARY networking

A Complete the sentences with words or phrases from the box.

contact	intern	job hunting	stay in touch
get to know	introduce yourself	make time for	

1 When you make friends with someone, you ________________ him or her.
2 When you say hello to someone for the first time, you ________________.
3 When you fit something into your schedule, you ________________ it.
4 An ________________ is someone who works for experience and usually isn't paid.
5 When you continue to communicate with an old friend, you ________________ with him or her.
6 When you are looking for work, you are ________________.
7 Someone you know in a profession is a ________________.

B IN PAIRS Discuss the questions.

1 Do you find it easy to introduce yourself to people and get to know them?
2 How can contacts help when you are job hunting or looking for a position as an intern?
3 Is it important to make time for old friends and stay in touch with them?

LISTENING

A Read the statement and say if you agree or disagree.

It's not what you know that's important—it's who you know.

B 12.03 LISTENING SKILL—Listen for the main ideas Listen to part of a radio show and check (✓) the advice the speaker gives.

- ☐ speak to people in your office
- ☐ speak to members of your family
- ☐ speak to old school friends
- ☐ join online groups
- ☐ research companies online
- ☐ go to career fairs
- ☐ write to companies

C 12.03 Listen again and complete the sentences with the words or short phrases you hear.

1 You can learn a lot from ________________ people in your office.
2 When you leave a job, it's a good idea to ________________ with people.
3 Ask questions, ________________, and post comments in online groups.
4 In online groups, you might be the first to hear about ________________.
5 You could ask companies about working as ________________.
6 In speed networking, you talk to each person for ________________.

D THINKING SKILL—Understand Explain how career fairs are useful.

GRAMMAR review of tenses

A Match the sentences (1–5) to the functions (a–e). Write the letter.

1 My contact **works** in the accounting department. ____
2 I **am looking** for an internship. ____
3 I **was** nervous about meeting people when I **started** working here. ____
4 I **was chatting** to a colleague when you **called** me. ____
5 **Have** you **spoken** to your friends about their career plans? ____

a a past state or habit
b an action in progress at a past moment
c a present state or habit
d an action in progress now
e an action at an unspecific time in the past

For more practice, go to page 159.

B Choose the correct option.

1 My plane … at six, so I'll be in Washington at nine.
 a leaves b has left c was leaving
2 Lola … as a waitress until she can find a job in engineering.
 a works b has worked c is working
3 I … to a speed networking event next weekend.
 a am going b have gone c go
4 If you … a professional association, you would make useful connections.
 a join b joined c have joined
5 I … in this office for six months.
 a work b am working c have worked

C Choose the correct option.

When I **1** have worked / was working at my last job, I **2** was trying / tried to speak to everyone in my office once a day. After I **3** was leaving / left that position, I **4** was staying / stayed in touch with all my colleagues. I **5** am thinking / think it's important because you never **6** know / have known when you might want someone's help. And it **7** has helped / was helping me a number of times. Right now, I **8** am looking / look for a new job, and I **9** ask / have asked my contacts about job opportunities. Fingers crossed!

SPEAKING

A IN PAIRS **Discuss the questions. Use the Confident Communicator box to help you.**

1 What are you thinking of doing to develop your network?
2 In what ways is networking important in your chosen profession?

B Check (✓) the things you personally are thinking of doing to develop your network. Then add details and other ideas.

☐ speak to family members
☐ speak to friends
☐ join online groups
☐ contact companies directly

______________________ ______________________

CONFIDENT COMMUNICATOR
START TALKING

To say how certain you are about a plan, use *probably* (*not*) or *definitely* (*not*):
I will definitely stay in touch with my friends.
I'll probably get a job as an intern.

Youth Subculture

VOCABULARY appearance

A Look at the pictures. Write the hairstyle or clothing style you think each person wears.

Hairstyle:
beard mustache short/long hair color

Clothing style:
dark/bright clothes jewelry earrings necklace tight/loose costume make-up

1

goth

____
____

2

hipster

____
____

3

otaku

____
____

B IN PAIRS Discuss the questions.

1 Do you prefer to wear bright or dark colors?
2 Do you have a particular clothing style? Is it similar to your friends' clothing style?
3 Do you generally wear accessories? Which ones?

MAKE IT YOURS

Think of the clothes and accessories you own. Do you know the English word for all of them? Check in a dictionary and make a note of any you don't know. Describe your personal style to a classmate.

LISTENING

A IN PAIRS Have you seen people who look like the pictures in VOCABULARY A, either in real life or on TV/online? Why do you think they dress in that style? Discuss.

B 12.04 LISTENING SKILL—Listen for gist Listen to a podcast and number the sentences in the correct order (1–4) to create a summary.

_____ Young people want to look different from their parents.
_____ Young people want to show their personality.
_____ Young people in different groups wear different clothes.
_____ Young people want to feel they belong to a group.

C 12.04 Listen again and write short answers.

1 What does the speaker say about goths?

____

2 What example of a youth subculture in the past does the speaker mention?

____

3 What might youth subcultures tell you about someone you've never met?

____

D THINKING SKILL—Understand Describe the youth subcultures that exist in your country. Discuss as a class.

WRITING a description

A Read the description and match the sentence halves. Write the letter.

One youth tribe in my country is cosplayers. A Japanese reporter invented the term *cosplay* using the words *costume* and *play* in 1984. Cosplayers are interested in video games. They create costumes based on characters from popular video games and movies. Cosplayers wear bright colors and often wear make-up to make them look like their favorite characters. They meet to show each other their colorful costumes, and they often take selfies to show people online. They often like listening to the music from video games. Personally, I think cosplayers are brave. They aren't afraid to dress like their heroes. Cosplaying is a great way to meet people with the same interests.

1 First, ____
2 Second, ____
3 Third, ____

a the writer gives his or her personal opinion.
b the writer gives background information and a little history.
c the writer describes what the people look like and what they do.

B You are going to write a description of a youth subculture. Make notes to answer the questions before you write.

1 What youth subculture are you going to write about? ____
2 What kind of clothes do they wear? ____
3 What do members do together? ____
4 Do they listen to a particular kind of music? ____
5 What is your opinion of that subculture? ____

C Write your description in your notebook. Be sure to include some history, a physical description, and your opinion.

SPEAKING

A Do you think it's a good idea or a bad idea to belong to a subculture? Make notes on why.

____

____

B IN PAIRS **Discuss the questions. Explain your reasons. Use the Confident Communicator box to help you.**

1 Do you think it's a good or a bad idea to belong to a subculture?
2 What are the advantages and the disadvantages?

CONFIDENT COMMUNICATOR
KEEP TALKING

To add a further point, say:
Also …
In addition to that, …
Not only that, but … also …
You can express your personality in a subculture. Not only that, but you can also meet people.

Language and Life

Media Literacy – Reaching a Target Group

A 12.05 **Read the article. Summarize how advertisers reach a particular target group. Write one sentence for each step in the process.**

REACHING A TARGET GROUP

Sometimes, a business has a product that it wants to sell to a certain group of people. For example, there is no point advertising a new car to people who don't drive. Governments, too, sometimes want to get information to a specific group. This might be information about children's health that they want to give to parents. In both cases, it would be a waste of money to inform everyone. It's better to aim your message at the people you want to reach. How do you do that?

First of all, it's important to clearly identify the group of people you want to reach. Is it parents? Is it teenagers? Is it homeowners? When you have a clear idea of your target group, then you can think about how to reach people in the group.

Second, you need to think about how to communicate with that group. Teenagers and young adults spend time on social networks. That might be the best way to reach them. It might not work so well for senior citizens or other groups.

Third, you need to express your message in the right way. With professional people, you may want to use serious language. With teenagers, you may want to use slang or informal language.

When you aim your message at a clear target group and use the right form of communication, your message is more effective.

1 ____________________

2 ____________________

3 ____________________

B IN PAIRS **Read the situation and say in your own words what you need to do.**

You work in the marketing department of a restaurant chain. Sales are slow and they want to get more customers. Your boss has asked you to think about some target customers and to suggest ways of advertising to them.

C **IN GROUPS** **Suggest what each group may want from a restaurant. Consider the elements from the list. Make notes below each picture.**

- Type of food
- Type of tables and chairs
- Type of music
- Special services

1

families with young children

____

____

2

teenagers

____

____

3

professional people

____

____

4

senior citizens

____

____

D **IN GROUPS** **Choose one group from C. Answer questions to design an advertisement to reach that group.**

1 Which group is your target group? ______________________________
2 What is the main thing they want from a restaurant? ______________________________
3 What is the best way to communicate with your target group? ______________________________
4 What kind of language will you use? ______________________________

E **IN GROUPS** **Design a poster, a TV ad, or an online post to communicate with your target group.**

F **IN GROUPS** **Share your ad with the class. Explain what you plan to do to reach your target group.**

G **Discuss the questions.**

1 Whose ad do you think would reach the target group best? Why?
2 In what other situations or jobs do you need to create ads?

MAKE IT DIGITAL

Research online for creative ways to reach members of your social group or the social group of someone you know.

VOCABULARY review

SCORE: / 10

A Circle the correct option.

1 Networking is a good way of **coming** / **getting** to know people in your profession.
2 I like wearing **loose** / **tight** clothes because they're more comfortable when it's hot.
3 It's important to **do** / **make** time for your family when you are busy at work.
4 Do you **belong** / **join** to any clubs?
5 In my company, we have meetings every morning to **share** / **tell** ideas.
6 My mom doesn't often wear rings, earrings, or other **jewelry** / **make-up**.
7 I'm job **hunting** / **looking** right now, so I'm writing to ask companies about vacancies.
8 Do you have any **contacts** / **interns** who can help me get a job in that company?
9 I like to **purpose** / **chat** with other students after class. It helps me make new friends.
10 My dad has a mustache, but he doesn't have a **beard** / **belt**.

GRAMMAR review

SCORE: / 10

A Complete the sentences with reflexive pronouns.

1 After the lecture, I introduced __________ to the speaker.
2 My brother hurt __________ in an accident.
3 I would rather do things __________ than have help from other people.
4 In an exam, make sure you give __________ enough time to check your answers.
5 Amy tried to tell __________ not to worry when she lost her job.

B Complete the sentences with the correct form of the verbs in parentheses.

1 How long __________ Mrs. Anderson? (you/know)
2 When you called, I __________ something on Netflix. (watch)
3 If you __________ a lot of money, what would you do with it? (find)
4 I __________ Matt, but he sounds like an interesting guy. (meet)
5 Sara __________ with her parents until she finds an apartment. (live)

16–20 correct: You can talk about networking and physical appearances. You can use reflexive pronouns.
0–15 correct: Look again at the Vocabulary and Grammar sections in the unit.

TOTAL SCORE: / 20

WHAT DO YOU KNOW NOW? Look back at page 117 and add the words you know now to the box.

FOLLOW A PRO BUSINESS

Take the quiz about business. Then go to **Follow A Pro** on page 138. Find the answers and learn more about business.

1 Which company was the first to be worth $1 trillion?
a Apple **b** Amazon **c** Microsoft

2 How many new businesses started up each month in the US during 2016?
a 50,000 **b** 250,000 **c** 550,000

3 Who is most comfortable with starting their own business?
a people over 35 **b** 25- to 35-year-olds **c** people under 25

4 According to a recent report, what is the best country to be an entrepreneur in?
a Japan **b** Germany **c** the US

STUDY SKILLS

A Read the two texts. Which is a personal narrative? Which is a factual account?

USING PERSONAL EXPERIENCE

1

Biggest Storm in 100 Years Hits the Country

Yesterday, strong winds of 100 kilometers per hour hit a popular coastal town. Businesses closed early, and buses and trains stopped running. By three p.m. yesterday afternoon, the streets were empty as people stayed inside. Hospitals, however, were very busy as over 100 people were injured by falling trees and flying debris. Luckily, no one was killed.

Sixty centimeters of rain fell in just 24 hours. Streets became rivers, and around 350 people had to leave their homes. Many buildings were damaged by the wind.

An estimated $25 million dollars will be required to repair the damage caused by this storm.

2

An Incredible Storm

I was on a camping trip with some friends. We were hiking in the state park when suddenly there was a huge storm. The sky turned black, and the wind became very strong. We started to feel really scared because we were far from the campground, and no one knew exactly where we were. We hiked back to the start of the trail, but it was really dangerous. Tree branches were breaking, and they almost hit us as they flew. When we arrived at the campground, there was no power, and there was water in the tent. Luckily, we found a hotel for the night. We were happy to be out of the storm!

B How can you tell factual accounts from personal narratives? Write *FA* (factual accounts) or *PN* (personal narratives).

1 _____ use words that describe feelings.
2 _____ often use the passive voice, e.g.: "Many homes were damaged."
3 _____ often use numbers, measurements, and percentages.
4 _____ usually tell stories.
5 _____ are objective.

C Match the columns to make sentences. What effect does it have when you combine fact and personal experience?

1 The earthquake of 2010 left 350,000 people homeless, _____
2 When the biggest music festival in the county took place, _____
3 At 4,810 meters, Mont Blanc is the highest mountain in Europe; _____
4 I think that Tokyo is one of the most exciting cities in the world, _____

a I was there, along with 500,000 other music lovers.
b and with a population of over 37 million, it's also the biggest.
c it is also the place where I learned to ski.
d including my mom, my dad, my brother, and me.

D In your notebook, combine the personal narrative and the factual account from A. Write a paragraph of about 100–125 words.

Remember:
- Don't overdo it. Two to three facts should be enough for a personal narrative.
- Choose the facts you add carefully. Use them only if they add impact to your writing.

When the biggest storm in 100 years hit the coastal area, I was hiking with my friends in the state park. We ...

E THINKING SKILL—Analyze **Where do you usually read personal accounts? Where do you usually read factual accounts? Which type of story is more interesting to you? Which is more truthful? Why?**

MAKE IT HAPPEN

Think of an exciting experience you have had. Write a paragraph about it, combining facts and personal experience.

Answers to the quiz on page 16
1 b and c 2 a 3 a and b

UNIT 2

FOLLOW A PRO

A Read about a hotel manager's job. Answer the questions below.

A HOTEL MANAGER

Albert Chaparro is the hotel manager for a large chain hotel in Lima, Peru. After graduating with a degree in business administration, he joined the chain's graduate training program. There, he learned how to apply his general business skills to the hospitality industry.

His role involves a wide range of activities. He might solve problems with the staff or check hotel supplies. He plays an important role in hiring and training staff, so he might interview applicants or train new workers. He has to manage both people and money.

His job also involves hotel services. He might arrange a large celebration for a group of business visitors. For this, he needs to work closely with the kitchen staff, in particular the head chef. They have to agree on a menu and a budget. During an important event, he monitors wait staff and makes sure everything runs according to plan.

He expects to continue in this job for a few more years. He hopes to get a higher position in hotel management, running a number of hotels in the same chain.

1 What did Albert study before training in hotel management? __________
2 What does Albert do with members of staff? __________
3 Who does Albert work closely with when arranging a celebration? __________
4 When does Albert make sure wait staff are following the plan correctly? __________
5 What does Albert expect to be doing in a few years? __________

B Discuss the questions as a class.

1 Do you think Albert's job is interesting? Why or why not?
2 What do you think is the hardest part of Albert's job?

VIDEO

WATCH THE VIDEO AND FOLLOW AN EVENT PLANNER.

C IN GROUPS Answer the questions.

1 What job is the video about? __________
2 What does the person do every day? __________
3 Does the person like the job? Why or why not? __________
4 What's the hardest part of the person's job? __________
5 What skills does the person need for the job? __________
6 What education or training did this person have? __________

D IN GROUPS Check your answers to the quiz on page 26 and discuss the questions.

1 Do you know people who work in hospitality?
2 What jobs in hospitality do you know?
3 How does knowing English help if you work in hospitality?
4 What personal qualities do you need to work in hospitality?
5 What opportunities to work in hospitality are there where you live?

Answers to the quiz on page 26
1 a 2 c 3 c

UNIT 3

STUDY SKILLS

A **A group of students is researching how college students watch entertainment at home. Read the questionnaire they wrote. Are the questions designed well? Why or why not?**

DESIGNING A QUESTIONNAIRE

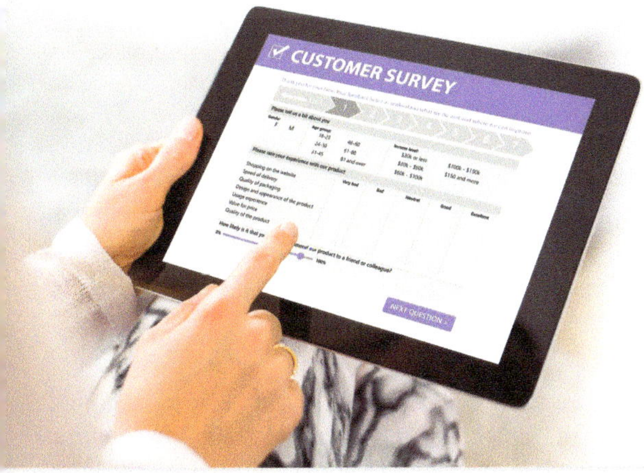

1 Which of the following best describes your job?
Full-time / Part-time

2 How many hours of TV do you watch per day?
Do you prefer series or movies on the internet?
Series / Movies

3 What do you think about reality shows?

4 I prefer to watch TV with friends.
a Strongly agree **b** Agree **c** Neither agree nor disagree
d Disagree **e** Strongly disagree

5 Do you ever lie about how much TV you watch?
Yes / No

B **Read the tips for designing questionnaires. Write the question numbers from A next to all the tips that can improve them. Then underline the questions from the questionnaire in A that follow the tips.**

a Use closed questions that have one answer only. You can count the answers quickly for your research. ______

b Make sure that your questions ask for just one piece of information. Don't ask two questions at the same time. ______

c Ask each question the same way. Use all questions or all statements. Write the answer choices in the same way, too. ______

d Make sure all your questions are on the topic you are researching. ______

e Make sure your questions don't embarrass or upset the people who might answer them. ______

C **Rewrite the questionnaire from A in your notebook. Use the tips to help you write good research questions. Write three more well-designed research questions. Ask about the following:**

6 channel surfing: ______?
______

7 binge-watching: ______?
______

8 how they feel about their TV watching habits: ______?
______

D **Write three well-designed survey questions to find out what snacks people eat when they're watching TV.**

E THINKING SKILL—Question **When might you use a questionnaire as part of a job? What jobs depend on getting accurate, useful information from questionnaires?**

MAKE IT HAPPEN

Design a questionnaire for a class, e.g., science, history, geography, or psychology. Decide on a research topic and write four to five questions to research it. Then ask your classmates to answer your questionnaire. Report the results to your class.

Answers to the quiz on page 36
1 a 2 a 3 b
(It's better to ask closed questions.)

UNIT 4 FOLLOW A PRO

A Read about a school psychologist's job. Answer the questions below.

A SCHOOL PSYCHOLOGIST

I'm Laura Cardoso and I work as a school psychologist. I work for the school district in a large city. I have a master's degree, and right now I'm working toward my PhD.

Children have different personalities, abilities, and needs. Most of them do fine in the educational system. However, some children need expert help. Some children find schoolwork hard, while other children are bored because their schoolwork doesn't challenge them enough. A school psychologist works with children to help them with their problems so that they can get the best education possible.

There are two main parts to my job. I work with children, parents, and teachers to plan a learning program for each child that needs help. I try to understand the personalities of the children I work with and any problems they have. I use my training to help them learn. The other part of my job involves training teachers in my city. I travel from school to school and explain common problems children have. It's very motivating to help children do their best.

1 What degree does Laura have? ______
2 Why do some children need a school psychologist? ______
3 Who does Laura work with when planning a learning program? ______
4 What does Laura do besides work with children? ______
5 What does Laura like about her job? ______

B Discuss the questions as a class.

1 Would you like to work as a school psychologist? Why or why not?
2 What skills are important for this job?

VIDEO

WATCH THE VIDEO AND FOLLOW A TEACHER.

C IN GROUPS Answer the questions.

1 What job is the video about? ______
2 Where does the person work? ______
3 Who does the person work with? ______
4 What special education does this person have? ______
5 Is the person happy in this job? ______
6 What does the person say is the best part of the job? ______

D IN GROUPS Check your answers to the quiz on page 46 and discuss the questions.

1 Do you know any people who work in education?
2 What other jobs in education do you know?
3 In what ways might English be useful for a psychologist in the field of education?
4 What personal qualities do you need to work in education?
5 What are the best and worst things about working in education?

Answers to the quiz on page 46
1 c 2 c 3 a

UNIT 5

STUDY SKILLS

A **Look at the study notes below for one minute. Try to memorize as many words as you can. Then close your book and write what you remember. Was the task hard? Why or why not?**

ORGANIZING TO HELP MEMORIZATION

Travel Vocabulary

book a flight
plane
check-in desk
go sightseeing
stay at a campsite
try the local specialties
check in at the airport
baggage claim
rent a vacation home
go through security
airplane
chill out on the beach
bus
take lots of pictures

B **Read the tips about organizing your notes for better memorization. Match the memorization tips (1–4) to the examples in the notes (a–d).**

1. Organize the words by category. ____
2. Write the words in short phrases. ____
3. Write a short sentence with some of the words. ____
4. Write several sentences that make a story with the words. ____

a *People in a Hotel*	*In the Room*	*Things to Ask the Receptionist*	*Verbs for Hotels*
valet	*king bed / queen bed / twin bed*	*Is breakfast included in the price?*	*book a room*
hotel receptionist	**b** *room with a balcony*	**d** *Can we get some extra towels, please?*	*check into the hotel*
housekeeping	*refrigerator*	*Could you recommend a good restaurant nearby?*	*check out of the hotel*
concierge	**c** *The room in Cancun was perfect. I got a room with a balcony so that I could look at the beach. There was a mini-fridge for snacks, but if I was very hungry, I called room service and ordered lunch.*		*call room service*

C **Organize the notes in A so that the words and phrases are easy to remember. Study them for one minute. Then write as many words as you can remember.**

Things to Do on Vacation

chill out on the beach

D **THINKING SKILL—Recall** **How do you organize information when you need to memorize facts for your classes? Do you organize information in a similar way when you study a language?**

MAKE IT HAPPEN

Choose one of the subjects you are studying now. Organize a vocabulary list for that subject so that the words are easier to memorize.

Answers to the quiz on page 56
Students' own answers.

UNIT 6

FOLLOW A PRO

A Read about the job of an ecological architect. Choose the option that is NOT correct.

AN ARCHITECT

Emilia Johnson is an architect in a company that specializes in ecological architecture. She completed her bachelor's degree in architecture and environmental design and then got a paid internship with the company. Four years later, she passed the Architect Registration Examination. She has worked at the company for eight years, and she plans to stay there for several more years.

Ecological architects design buildings that are a natural part of the world. They design buildings that use natural resources, such as solar energy. They also design buildings with natural materials, such as a green roof (plants growing on top of a building). Emilia works with civil engineers and interior designers to make sure that her designs have a positive impact on the environment. She explains her designs to urban planners so that her buildings can become part of a larger plan for a city.

Emilia needs good technical skills and creativity. She has to make beautiful buildings that are also water and energy-efficient. She visualizes the design of the project and then creates drawings using CAD (Computer Aided Design) software. She checks that construction workers are following her design.

Emilia loves being an ecological architect. The best part of her job is seeing her clients living and working happily in a building that fits in the world naturally.

1 For four years, Emilia worked as an intern / as a volunteer / before passing an exam / on ecological buildings.
2 Ecological architects create buildings with natural materials / solar panels / plants / plastic roofs.
3 Emilia's designs are used by engineers and designers / created on computers / made by clients / explained to urban planners.
4 Ecological architects need good marketing / communication / technical / creative skills.

B Discuss the questions as a class.

1 Do you think it is important to create ecological architecture? Why or why not?
2 How can architects help make buildings more ecological?
3 Have you been in any buildings that are "green"? How do those buildings save water or energy?

VIDEO

WATCH THE VIDEO AND FOLLOW AN URBAN PLANNER.

C IN GROUPS Answer the questions.

1 What job is the video about? ______________________
2 What are the person's working hours? ______________________
3 What are some of the good and bad things about the job? ______________________
____
4 Is the person's job hard? Why or why not? ______________________
____
5 What skills does the person use at this job? ______________________
____

D IN GROUPS Check your answers to the quiz on page 66 and discuss the questions.

1 What other jobs in architecture do you know?
2 Do you need English to be an architect?
3 What personal qualities do you need for this job?
4 Are there opportunities in the field of architecture in your country?

Answers to the quiz on page 66
1 c 2 b 3 a 4 c

A **Look at two personal narratives. Which story is more interesting, in your opinion? Why?**

CREATIVITY

My First Day of College

I was a little nervous on my first day of college. I got lost on campus, and it took me half an hour to find my class. The professor seemed irritated that I arrived late, and I felt really stressed. I was lost and lonely because I didn't know anyone at the college. I didn't really need to worry because the other students were very nice. I'm still good friends with some of the people from my first day. The teachers here are very nice, too, and now I can find my way around the campus easily.

By Sebastian

My First Day of College

The college campus looked like a different planet. It felt light-years away from Earth and everything was unfamiliar. Finding my class on the first day was like going to the moon. It seemed like I was walking around in circles. I hunted for the classroom for half an hour before I landed there. I was a lonely alien in a crazy, crowded campus. Fortunately, the other life-forms on the planet were fun-loving and peaceful and became my new friends. After some time, everything became less strange.

By Elsa

B **Read Elsa's story again. What words does she choose to describe ...**

1 the college campus? ______________________________

2 how she arrived in class? ______________________________

3 the other students? ______________________________

4 how she felt? ______________________________

C **IN PAIRS Read the definitions of a simile and a metaphor. Then write similes or metaphors to describe the things below.**

Simile: When you compare two things, saying that one is like another, e.g.: "The college campus looked like a different planet."
Metaphor: When you describe something as being something different (to show the similarities between the two things), e.g.: "I was a lonely alien."

1 falling in love ______________________________

2 a stressful exam ______________________________

3 a family party ______________________________

4 a pet you love ______________________________

D **Choose one of the ideas in C and write a paragraph. Use the simile or metaphor in your paragraph to make your writing interesting.**

My dog Laika is a hurricane. When she rushes into the room, there's noise, and nothing is safe ...

E **THINKING SKILL—Brainstorm In what ways are you creative? Do you enjoy expressing your feelings, solving problems, or inventing things? How can you use your creative gift in your life or work?**

MAKE IT HAPPEN

Keep a notebook of things you want to write about.
Then choose one of the topics to write an essay about.

Answers to the quiz on page 76
1 c 2 b (It makes you more creative.) 3 b 4 b

UNIT 8

FOLLOW A PRO

A Read about a resort activities coordinator's job. Choose *True* or *False* below.

A RESORT ACTIVITIES COORDINATOR

Sergio Herrero is an activities coordinator at a large resort hotel in Costa Rica. He plans and directs sports and entertainment activities for children and adults, and he takes guests on nature walks along the beach. Sergio also coordinates the activities section on the hotel's website and helps manage the budget for his department.

Sergio is 24, and he has a degree in hotel management. He says that getting a management job right after graduation is very hard, and being an activities coordinator gives him some experience working for a large hotel. Sergio says the salary isn't great, but his expenses are low. He lives at the hotel and eats his meals there for free. Guests often tip the activities coordinators, and that's always nice!

Sergio says that an activities coordinator should have a college degree in a field like hotel management, sales and marketing, or sports management. It's important to speak English and one other language, especially at international resorts. And having the right personality is essential. Activities coordinators have to love people. They have to be friendly and enthusiastic, and they have to know how to play games and sports, and even sing or dance.

Sergio is enjoying his job and learning a lot about the hotel business. He says he especially likes meeting people from many different places around the world.

1 Entertaining guests is Sergio's only job responsibility. True / False
2 Sergio is working as an activities coordinator to get experience in hotel work. True / False
3 Being an activities coordinator has some benefits apart from the salary. True / False
4 You only have to speak one language to be an activities coordinator. True / False
5 Activities coordinators work with people of all ages. True / False
6 Sergio thinks that being an activities coordinator is a good way to enter the hotel business. True / False

B Discuss the questions as a class.

1 Is an activities coordinator's job important? Why or why not?
2 Have you ever seen an activities coordinator working? If so, tell the class about what you observed.
3 Would you like to be an activities coordinator? Why or why not?

VIDEO

WATCH THE VIDEO AND FOLLOW A RECREATION COORDINATOR.

C IN GROUPS Answer the questions.

1 What job is the video about? ______________________
2 What does the person do every day? ______________________
____
3 What is interesting about this job? ______________________
____
4 Does this person work long hours? ______________________
5 Is the person satisfied with the job? ______________________
6 Is there anything the person doesn't like? ______________________

D IN GROUPS Check your answers to the quiz on page 86 and discuss the questions.

1 Do you think you have the right qualifications to work as an activities coordinator?
2 What are some advantages and disadvantages of working as an activities coordinator?
3 What other leisure industry jobs can you think of?
4 What leisure industry jobs would be interesting to you?
5 What qualifications do you need to work in different jobs in the leisure industry?

Answers to the quiz on page 86
1 c 2 b 3 a, b, c, d, e

STUDY SKILLS

A Read the conversation about a group of students working on a research project. Are the students using good problem-solving skills? Why or why not?

PROBLEM SOLVING

Carla: For our group assignment, we have to offer solutions to the lack of safe, affordable, and quick transportation to the college. It says here that we need to present three ideas for transportation, outlining the advantages and disadvantages of each idea.
Bobby: Right. Well, that's easy. Let's present an idea for a college taxi service. That's all we need!
Maggie: Yeah, it's safe, affordable, and it would be quick, too! Nice job. We're done!
Carla: Hold on! We're not finished yet. We need three different ideas, not just one.
Bobby: Oh, I forgot about that. So, we've already got a taxi service. How about self-driving taxis, too?
Carla: Yeah, OK. And maybe ride sharing, too?
Maggie: Yes. And why don't we find out how most students get to college in a typical week?
Bobby: Good idea. I'll ask my friends, OK? That'll be quick. That can be my part, and you can do all the other stuff.
Carla: No, we need to do more research than that! And we probably need to write a report. What do you think?
Maggie: Is that necessary? Can't we all just say what we want in a presentation?
Bobby: Yeah, that's probably the best plan.
Carla: Hmm … I'm not sure that's enough.
Maggie: Well, if you think we need a report, you can write it.

B Choose all the correct answers about the conversation in A.

The students aren't using good problem-solving skills because …

1 They haven't divided the work equally.
2 They aren't thinking about how to effectively research the problem.
3 They haven't considered several different solutions before deciding on three.
4 They haven't decided on a good way to research their topic.
5 They aren't sure if they have to write a report or just give the presentation.

C Number the steps in the problem-solving process in the correct order (1–4).

_____ Write down how you managed to solve the problem.
_____ Read the task carefully and make sure you understand it.
_____ Look at the problem in a few different ways. Think about many possible solutions.
_____ Decide what information you need to help you solve the problem.

D In your notebook, rewrite the conversation in A using your ideas and the problem-solving tips in C. Show good problem-solving skills.

E THINKING SKILL—Evaluate Employers look for employees who can help solve problems. What qualities does a good problem-solver have? Make a list.

Listens to everyone's opinion, …

MAKE IT HAPPEN

Apply some of the problem-solving techniques you have learned to your own studies or work. Keep a journal about the process you used to solve a problem and decide what helped you reach a solution.

Answers to the quiz on page 96
1 a, b, c 2 a and c

UNIT 10 FOLLOW A PRO

A **Read about a family physician's job. Answer the questions below.**

A FAMILY PHYSICIAN

There are many different kinds of doctors. Grace Lincoln is a family physician.

"I always wanted to be a doctor from the time I was very young. I took a lot of science classes in high school and then majored in biology in college. I took anatomy, biology, and chemistry—all classes that are in a pre-med curriculum. After that, I went to medical school for four years and then had four more years of practical training before I got my present job. It's a long, hard road, but I can't imagine doing anything else.

"I use a lot of different skills every day. I need medical knowledge, of course, but I also need to be good with people. When my patients are ill or injured, they need the right treatment, but they also need to know that I understand how they feel. And I have to be ready for anything. My next patient might be an elderly person with a broken arm or a child with a fever. I love the feeling that I'm making a real difference in people's lives."

1 What kind of doctor is Grace? ____________
2 When did Grace first want to be a doctor? ____________
3 What was Grace's major as an undergraduate? ____________
4 How many years of medical school and training did Grace complete before she got her job?
____
5 What does Grace like about her job? ____________

B **Discuss the questions as a class.**

1 Would you like to be a doctor?
2 What do you think is the best part of being a doctor?

VIDEO

WATCH THE VIDEO AND FOLLOW A PHYSICAL THERAPIST.

C **IN GROUPS Answer the questions.**

1 What job is the video about? ____________
2 What special skills or education does this person have? ____________
____
3 Who does the person work with? ____________
4 What are some of the good and bad things about the job? ____________
____
5 Is the person's job hard? Why or why not? ____________
____
6 Does this person need multiple languages to do this job? ____________

D **IN GROUPS Check your answers to the quiz on page 106 and discuss the questions.**

1 Do you know anybody who works in health care?
2 How does someone become a doctor in your country?
3 What skills do you think a doctor needs?
4 Do men and women do the same jobs in health care in your country?
5 What area of health care would you most like to work in?

Answers to the quiz on page 106
1 c 2 a 3 c

UNIT 11

STUDY SKILLS

A **Yadira is working on an essay for her science class. Read her notes and her paragraph. Has she used all of the facts in her writing? Underline the words she should replace with precise facts.**

USING PRECISE LANGUAGE IN ACADEMIC WRITING

Research Notes

- *70% of the Earth is covered in water*
- *less than 3% of the Earth's water is fresh water*
- *17% of people don't have clean drinking water*
- *cholera and dysentery are diseases caused by unclean water*
- *in developing countries, 80% of illnesses are caused by dirty drinking water*

How can we help more people have clean drinking water?

Most of the world's surface is covered by water, but not much of it is fresh. Many people have no access to clean water and this is really terrible. Clean water is very important for our health, and it is also important for keeping everything clean. Unclean drinking water causes some serious diseases, such as cholera and dysentery. These diseases stop people from working and cause economic problems. I think it's terrible that rich countries don't do more about this.

B **Read the tips on writing academic essays. Then rewrite the sentences with more precise language.**

- Use specific facts in your writing and be precise in your language. Look for statistics from reliable sources, such as books, journals, and trusted internet sites.
- Don't use generalizations (a lot of people say … , no one wants … , more people prefer …).
- Opinions are your personal beliefs. Don't give opinions in academic essays unless you also have facts to support your opinions.

1 Many students in my English class have studied English for more than a year.

____

2 Some students take a class in the morning, and some take a class at night.

____

3 I like taking a class at night because I don't like getting up early in the morning.

____

4 A face-to-face class is more fun than an online class. That's why a lot of students prefer to attend a class.

____

C **In your notebook, rewrite Yadira's paragraph in A using the tips for academic writing in B.**

D THINKING SKILL—Apply **Why is it important to know how to be precise in your writing? How could remembering these tips help you to be a better writer?**

MAKE IT HAPPEN

Choose a topic from your work or studies. Research facts about the topic and write a paragraph in academic style. Use data and precise language to explain the topic.

Answers to the quiz on page 116
1 b 2 b 3 a 4 b

UNIT 12

FOLLOW A PRO

A Read about an entrepreneur's job. Answer the questions below.

AN ENTREPRENEUR

I'm Juana Geller. I run my own ethical jewelry business. My company designs and sells jewelry made from eco-friendly materials. I started my business when I was a teenager. I wanted to buy and wear jewelry that was different from everyone else. I made necklaces from glass beads. My friends liked my designs, so I started making necklaces and selling them to friends and family.

After high school, I learned about eco-friendly jewelry. I attended workshops on materials that could be recycled. I worked very hard and did a lot of networking. I visited many stores and talked about my ideas. A few stores decided to sell my jewelry, and the managers gave me advice on running my business. Young people liked my jewelry and talked about it on social media. The business started to grow, and I decided to get a degree in business administration to help me run it better.

Today, my company employs 50 people, and our jewelry is in stores across the country. We also sell a lot online. To be successful as an entrepreneur, you need to be able to take risks and be confident while you do it. You won't get much sleep for the first few years, but with a little luck, it'll be worth it in the end!

1 What does Juana's company produce? ______________________
2 Why did Juana start her business? ______________________
3 How did Juana get started? ______________________
4 What qualifications does Juana have? ______________________
5 What does Juana say about being a successful entrepreneur? ______________________

____

B Discuss the questions as a class.

1 Is being self-employed a good idea? Why or why not?
2 Can you imagine being self-employed?

VIDEO

WATCH THE VIDEO AND FOLLOW AN ENTREPRENEUR.

C IN GROUPS Answer the questions.

1 What kind of job does this person do? ______________________
2 Where does this person work? ______________________
3 What are the person's working hours? ______________________
4 What special skills does this person need? ______________________
5 How did this person learn the skills for the job? ______________________
6 Why do you think this person likes his job? ______________________

D IN GROUPS Check your answers to the quiz on page 126 and discuss the questions.

1 Do you know people who have started their own businesses?
2 Would you like to start your own business? Why or why not?
3 What are the risks of starting your own business?
4 In what ways would English help in starting your own business?
5 What skills does an entrepreneur need?

Answers to the quiz on page 126
1 a 2 c 3 c 4 b (Japan was second and the US was third.)

Irregular Verbs

Infinitive	Simple past	Past participle
be	was/were	been
become	became	become
begin	began	begun
break	broke	broken
bring	brought	brought
build	built	built
buy	bought	bought
catch	caught	caught
choose	chose	chosen
come	came	come
cost	cost	cost
cut	cut	cut
do	did	done
draw	drew	drawn
drink	drank	drunk
drive	drove	driven
eat	ate	eaten
fall	fell	fallen
feed	fed	fed
feel	felt	felt
find	found	found
fly	flew	flown
get	got	gotten
give	gave	given
go	went	gone
grow	grew	grown
hang	hung	hung
have	had	had
hear	heard	heard
hit	hit	hit
hold	held	held
hurt	hurt	hurt
keep	kept	kept
know	knew	known
leave	left	left
let	let	let
lose	lost	lost
make	made	made
meet	met	met
pay	paid	paid
put	put	put
read	read	read
ride	rode	ridden
ring	rang	rung
rise	rose	risen
run	ran	run
say	said	said
see	saw	seen
sell	sold	sold
send	sent	sent
set	set	set
sing	sang	sung
sit	sat	sat
speak	spoke	spoken
stand	stood	stood
stick	stuck	stuck
take	took	taken
teach	taught	taught
tell	told	told
think	thought	thought
throw	threw	thrown
understand	understood	understood
wake	woke	woken
wear	wore	worn
win	won	won
write	wrote	written

Pronunciation Symbols

Vowels

ɪ	d**i**d
ɛ	b**e**d
æ	b**a**d
ʌ	c**u**p
ʊ	b**oo**k
ə	banan**a**
i	f**ee**d
ɑ	f**a**ther, b**o**x
ɔ	t**a**ll
u	st**u**dent, f**oo**d
ɝ	sh**ir**t, b**ir**thday
eɪ	d**a**te, t**a**ble
aɪ	cr**y**, **ey**e
ɔɪ	b**oy**
oʊ	c**o**mb, p**o**st
aʊ	ab**ou**t, h**ow**

Consonants

p	**p**ark, ha**pp**y
b	**b**ack, ho**bb**y
t	**t**ea
d	**d**ie
k	**c**ame, **k**itchen, **q**uarter
g	**g**ame, **g**o
f	**f**ace, **ph**otographer
V	**v**egetable
θ	**th**ing, ma**th**
ð	**th**en, **th**at
s	**c**ity, **s**ummer
z	plea**s**e, goe**s**
ʃ	**sh**e, **sh**op
ʒ	lei**s**ure
h	**h**ot, **wh**o
tʃ	**ch**icken, wa**tch**
dʒ	**j**acket, oran**g**e
m	**m**en
n	su**n**, **kn**ow
ŋ	su**ng**, si**ng**er
w	**w**eek, **wh**ite
r	**r**ain, **wr**iter
l	**l**ight, **l**ong
j	**y**es, **u**se, m**u**sic

Grammar Review

A Match the questions (1–8) to the answers (a–h). Write the letter.

1 Do you like using social media? ____
2 How's it going? ____
3 Who do you live with? ____
4 When do you start work? ____
5 Is there a library in your town? ____
6 Can you run fast? ____
7 How much milk do we have? ____
8 Did he do his homework? ____

a We have half a liter.
b At 9 a.m.
c No, I can't!
d Good, thanks.
e No, there isn't.
f My parents and my brother.
g Yes, I do.
h Yes, he did.

B Complete the sentences with the phrases from the box.

has to | like to | need to | plan to | want to | would like to

1 Next year, I really ____________ travel the world.
2 ____________ you ____________ come with me?
3 I ____________ plan my trip before I go.
4 My passport ____________ be up to date.
5 I ____________ be away for about a year.
6 I ____________ travel. It's one of my favorite things.

C Complete simple past sentences using the verbs in parentheses.

1 Last weekend, I ____________ (celebrate) my birthday with family and friends.
2 We ____________ (go) to my favorite restaurant.
3 I ____________ (not have) a party at my home because my apartment is too small.
4 The meal ____________ (be) delicious, and we all really ____________ (enjoy) it.
5 We ____________ (not go) to a movie because it was so late when we finished dinner.
6 What ____________ (do) you do last weekend?

D Complete the conversation with the comparative form of the adjectives in parentheses.

Tim: Where do you want to eat this weekend? Do you want to go to the pizza place or the new restaurant?
Lara: Hmm, I don't know. The pizza place is **1** ____________ (cheap).
Tim: Yes, but I think the food at the new place is **2** ____________ (good). Their salads look good, too. I think you get **3** ____________ (healthy) food there.
Lara: You're probably right. I'm not sure about the staff at the new place. I think the waiters at the pizza place are **4** ____________ (friendly).
Tim: So many people are talking about the new restaurant, though! It's **5** ____________ (popular) than the pizza place.
Lara: Yes, but the pizza place is **6** ____________ (close), and it's raining.

E Rewrite the sentences correctly.

1 She can run really fastly. ______________________________

2 She speaks English good. ______________________________

3 Can you more slowly speak, please? ______________________________

4 You need to do very carefully this. ______________________________

5 He caught the ball easy. ______________________________

6 He studied hardly for his exam. ______________________________

F Read and choose the correct option.

I really love my hometown. **1** There are / There is a lot of nice restaurants and **2** there are / there is some small cafés, too. **3** There is / There are a big library, and **4** there's / there are a school. **5** There aren't / There isn't too many stores, but there is a beautiful park. What about your town? **6** Are there / Is there a lot of things to do?

G Complete the sentences with the present progressive form of the words in parentheses.

1 Rory ______________________ (take) a selfie.

2 Sula ______________________ (update) her profile.

3 Jan ______________________ (post) comments on a blog.

4 Manny and Luca ______________________ (send) texts to each other.

5 Mary's video ______________________ (go) viral.

6 Everyone ______________________ (look) at their screens.

7 They ______________________ (not speak) to each other.

H Read and choose the correct option.

Ava: Can I have **1** some / a milk, please?
Will: Of course. **2** How much / How many do you want?
Ava: I'd like a liter, please. Can I have **3** this / some apples, too?
Will: Sure. **4** These / This red ones?
Ava: No, **5** those / that green ones, please.
Will: Here you go.
Ava: **6** How much / How many is that, please?

UNIT 1 — past progressive

Function

We use the past progressive to talk about an action that began in the past and continued for some time.

Form

Affirmative		Negative	
I was	watching TV.	I wasn't	watching TV.
You were	studying English.	You weren't	studying English.
He was She was It was	playing video games. learning the guitar. raining.	He wasn't She wasn't It wasn't	playing video games. learning the guitar. raining.
We were	listening to music.	We weren't	listening to music.
They were	dancing together.	They weren't	dancing together.

Yes/No questions		Affirmative short answer	Negative short answer
Was I	sleeping?	Yes, I was.	No, I wasn't.
Were you	listening?	Yes, you were.	No, you weren't.
Was he Was she Was it	cooking? singing? snowing?	Yes, he was. Yes, she was. Yes, it was.	No, he wasn't. No, she wasn't. No, it wasn't.
Were we	working?	Yes, we were.	No, we weren't.
Were they	running?	Yes, they were.	No, they weren't.

UNIT 1 — past progressive vs. simple past

Function

We use the past progressive to describe an action in progress, and the simple past to introduce an interrupting action.

Form

Action in progress	Interrupting action
I was eating a sandwich	when my phone rang.
We were running a marathon	when it started raining.
She was out shopping	when she met a friend.
Were you watching TV	when you heard the news?

Interrupting action	Action in progress
The fire broke out	while they were sleeping.
The accident happened	while my brother was driving.
When I woke up,	it was raining.
Where were you	while this was happening?

A Read the conversation and choose the correct option.

Marta: What **1 were / was** you doing last night? Did you see the match on TV?
Sam: No, I didn't. I **2 was reading / read** a book. It was so good I forgot about the match!
Marta: What was the book about?
Sam: It's a biography about an artist in New York. When he was a child, he was always drawing and **3 painted / painting**. Then one day, when he was playing in the street, a car **4 hit / was hitting** him. He was badly hurt. While he was in the hospital, a nurse **5 gave / was giving** him a book about art. This book made him want to become an artist. Then years later, he **6 was drawing / drew** in the park when he **7 was seeing / saw** the nurse who gave him the book. While they **8 talked / were talking**, he drew her a picture to say thank you.
Marta: Wow! I bet that picture's worth millions of dollars now!

B Complete the sentences with the present progressive or the past tense form of the words in parentheses.

1. Anna ______________ (watch) the sunset when she decided to start her own business. The first thing she needed was some money.
2. When she ______________ (call) her bank, the bank manager was speaking to another customer.
3. Anna ______________ (write) her business plan when the bank manager returned her call.
4. While they ______________ (discuss) Anna's idea, her friend Greta came into the room.
5. Greta ______________ (ask) who Anna was talking to.
6. Anna was explaining her business plan to her friend when she ______________ (get) an email from the bank manager saying the bank could lend her the money.

UNIT 2 — quantifiers: *some, any, too much/many, a lot of, a little, a few*

Function

We use quantifiers to talk about amounts. Some quantifiers go with countable nouns, some go with uncountable nouns, and some go with both.

Form

Countable	Uncountable	Both
a few too many	a little too much	some any a lot of

A Identify the mistakes and rewrite the sentences correctly.

1. There's only a few milk in the refrigerator.
   ____
2. I think there's too many salt in this meal.
   ____
3. You need a lot tomatoes to make tomato soup.
   ____
4. Can you please buy me a little apples when you're at the store?
   ____
5. Don't eat too many candy! It's not good for you.
   ____
6. Can I have some grape, please?
   ____

B Choose the correct option.

At the end of winter, **1** **a lot of** / **a little** people around the world celebrate the end of cold, dark days. **2** **Some** / **A little** towns and villages do this by having street parties and making fires. On the Scottish island of Shetland, there is a fire festival every January. At that time of year, it's really cold and there's only **3** **a little** / **a few** daylight. Not **4** **too many** / **too much** people live in Shetland, but the party is huge! I wanted to go to the fire festival last year, but the flights cost **5** **too much** / **too many** money. I'm saving money now, and I plan to go there next year with **6** **a few** / **a little** friends.

UNIT 2 — *enough / not enough*

Function

We use *enough* to show that something is the right amount. *Not enough* shows that something is not the right amount. We use *enough* with countable and uncountable nouns.

Form

Countable	Uncountable
There are enough apples. We don't have enough books. There aren't enough cookies. Not enough people know about it. Do we have enough chairs?	She has enough money. They don't have enough clothes. There is enough milk. There is not enough time to finish the test. Is there enough room?

A Unscramble and write the sentences.

1 enough / this / have / we / do / food / for / party / ?

____

2 I / think / have / enough / we / .

____

3 enough / we / really / do / have / pizza / ?

____

4 enough / we / pizza / have / .

____

5 chairs / there / are / enough / ?

____

6 don't / enough / to / more / chairs / get / we / have / time / !

____

UNIT 3 — indefinite pronouns: *any, some, no, every + one/body/thing/where*

Form and function

We use indefinite pronouns when we are talking about a thing, person, or amount in a nonspecific way.
Use *any–* in questions or negative statements. *I don't want to do anything.*
Any– is used when it's not certain if a person, place, or thing exists. *Is anyone there?*
Any– is also used to refer to all persons, places, or things. *Anyone can do it.*

Indefinite pronoun	Means …	Example
everything	all things	I love everything about Paris!
everybody	all people	Everybody likes Anna.
everyone	all people	Everyone knows you.
everywhere	all places	They go everywhere together.
nothing	no things	There was nothing in his wallet.
nobody	no people	Nobody told me the news.
no one	no people	No one lives here.
nowhere	no places	This is like nowhere on Earth.
something	an unknown thing	I think I heard something.
somebody	an unknown person	Somebody heard us. Run!
someone	an unknown person	Someone is watching them.
somewhere	an unknown place	I need to go somewhere quiet.
anything	non-specific things	Can you see anything?
anybody	non-specific people	I don't know anybody here!
anyone	non-specific people	There isn't anyone I can ask.
anywhere	non-specific place	Is there anywhere we can go?

A Complete the text with indefinite pronouns from the box.

anyone anyone everyone no one something something

Last summer, I wanted to do **1** ____________ a little different for my vacation. My friends were all away, and there was **2** ____________ to hang out with. **3** ____________ was posting on social media about what a cool time they were having, so I decided to do **4** ____________ cool, too. I joined a summer camp for young people who wanted to learn about the art of street entertaining. At first, I felt nervous because I didn't know **5** ____________ there. After a few days, I loved it. I learned how to juggle and also learned some neat magic tricks. Did **6** ____________ have as good a vacation as I did? I doubt it!

B Identify the mistakes and rewrite the sentences correctly.

1 When I first moved here, I didn't know someone. ____________

2 Anyone seemed to have their own friends, so it was hard to meet people.
____

3 I felt lonely and decided I needed to do anything about it.
____

4 I looked around everything for clubs I could join. ____________

5 Finally, I found anything I was interested in—a video gaming club.
____

6 I really love this club. Someone is so friendly! ____________

UNIT 3 — *used to*

Function

We use *used to* to describe a habitual past action that isn't happening now.

Form

Affirmative			Negative		
I You He/She It We They	used to	live here. do ballet. play football. take a long time. go there. be friends.	I You He/She It We They	didn't use to	like it, but now I love it. recycle, but now you do. exercise, but now he/she runs marathons. work, but I just fixed it. hang out, but now we meet every weekend. play soccer, but now they're good at it.

Questions			
Did	I you he/she it we they	use to	make up songs as a child? work there? go running? play music? go there often? live here?

A Identify the mistakes and rewrite the sentences correctly.

1 Did your brother used to singing in a band? ______
2 He use to be the lead singer of a hard rock band. ______
3 I didn't used to like hard rock, but now I love it. ______
4 Did you used take a music class at school? ______
5 Yeah, I used taking one, but I stopped! It was a lot of extra work.
______
6 You should try again. There's a different teacher now. The last teacher use to make us work too hard!
______

B Choose the correct option.

1 The café we **used to** / **use to** eat in is now a really cool clothes shop.
2 He **use to** / **didn't use to** wear nice clothes, but now he looks great!
3 I **didn't use to** / **didn't used to** speak English, but now I do.
4 Did they **use to** / **used to** be friends? They don't talk to each other now.
5 My sister **used to** / **use to** be a teacher, but now she's a business owner.
6 He **didn't use to** / **used to** eat fast food all the time, but now he eats very healthily.
7 Did you **use to** / **used to** live here? I think I recognize you from somewhere.

UNIT 4 — comparative review and *(not) as … as*

Function

We use comparatives to compare one thing, person, or place to another thing, person, or place. We use *as … as* to show that two things are equal. We use *(not) as … as* to show that two things are not equal.

Form

Adjectives with one syllable	Adjectives that end with –y and have two syllables
My sister is quieter than I am. Silvia is nicer than Ella.	Horacio is happier than Frank. I'm lazier than my sister is.

Adjectives with two or more syllables	Irregular forms
Cities are more expensive than small towns. He is more handsome than his father. Now I'm more ambitious than I was then.	He's a better cook than his sister is. New York is farther from her than Chicago is.

as … as	*(not) as … as*
She's as friendly as her daughter. He's as tall as I am. I'm as stressed as you are about this.	I'm not as creative as you are. They're not as hard-working as we are. She's not as optimistic as she used to be.

A Choose the correct option.

My brother and I are twins—we look very similar, except that I'm **1 as tall as / not as tall as** he is. I'm only 175 centimeters! We both have blue eyes, although I think his eyes **2 are bluer / are more bluer**. When it comes to personality, we're really different. I don't think he's **3 as serious as / not as serious as** I am. He's **4 more sociable / sociabler** than I am and likes hanging out with his friends, while I like to be alone. I'd like to be **5 as easygoing / not as easygoing** as he is, but I wouldn't like to be **6 as lazy / not as lazy** as he is!

B Correct the mistakes.

1 I think that the coffee in this café is more good than the other one. ______
2 A city vacation is expensiver than a vacation in the country. ______
3 Our apartment isn't modern as yours. ______
4 Is your homework as hard like mine? ______
5 Her driving isn't getting better. It's getting badder! ______
6 You should do this task first because it's importanter. ______
7 Tom was as happy than you when he heard the news. ______

UNIT 4 — superlative adjectives

Function

We use superlatives to compare more than two things.

Form

Adjectives with one syllable	Adjectives that end with –y and have two syllables
It's the cheapest restaurant in town. What's the quickest way to get there? It's the smallest room in the house.	She's the funniest girl in the class. That was the happiest day of my life. July is the sunniest month in my country.

Adjectives with two or more syllables	Irregular forms
He's the most interesting man I've ever met. I think she's the most confident student. You're the most patient teacher in the school.	This is the best holiday ever! I've had the worst day. I think she ran the farthest.

A Complete the conversation with the superlative form of the adjectives in parentheses.

Sue: I'm organizing the end-of-year awards, Robert. Can you help me?
Robert: Well, I know what you should get the prize for, Sue—**1** ______ (hardworking) student in the school!
Sue: Aw, thanks, Robert! We don't have that category this year, though. There is a prize for **2** ______ (easygoing) person in our grade. Who should that be?
Robert: Hmm, what about Donato? He doesn't really do anything at all. He could win the prize for **3** ______ (lazy) guy, maybe?
Sue: That wouldn't be very nice! I also need to find someone to win the prize for **4** ______ (creative) idea of the year.
Robert: What about Daniella's charity fashion show? That was really creative.
Sue: Ah, yes, good idea. There's also a prize for **5** ______ (good) team worker …
Robert: Oh, that should be Nick. He likes everyone. You know, I really think he's **6** ______ (nice) guy in the whole school.

UNIT 5 — modals of intention, offer, and prediction

Function and form

We use modal verbs *will/won't* to state our intentions, make and refuse offers, and make predictions. We also use *can/can't* to make and refuse offers.

	Intention	Prediction
affirmative	I'll check out at 10 a.m. We'll go sightseeing today.	It'll rain tomorrow! We'll be there in three hours.
negative	I won't stay late. We won't stay here again.	There won't be any free rooms. We won't get there in time.

Make an offer	Refuse an offer
I'll help you with that! Can you stay for dinner? We can go sightseeing today.	No thanks, I won't need help. I can't stay any longer. I can't today, maybe tomorrow.

A Choose the correct option.

Receptionist: Hi, welcome to City Hostel! **1 Can / Will** I help you?
Sandor: Hi! My name is Sandor Vargas. I've booked three nights here—but it looks so lovely here that I think **2 I'll / I can** stay a little longer.
Receptionist: Great! **3 Will / Won't** you extend your reservation by another night, then? **4 I'll / I won't** check our availability.
Sandor: Thanks.
Receptionist: That's fine. We **5 will / won't** be very busy for the next few nights. It's often quiet at this time of year. So, here's your key card. Breakfast is from 6 to 8 a.m.
Sandor: Great. I'm really tired, so I probably **6 will / won't** go to breakfast tomorrow.

B Complete the sentences with words from the box.

can 'll 'll will will won't won't

1 ______________ you come to my birthday party next Friday?
2 It ______________ be easy to study and work part time in the café. It's too much!
3 ______________ I help you carry your bags? They look heavy.
4 I ______________ be a little late getting home today because I have a dentist appointment after school.
5 ______________ you stay and have dinner with us? We're having pizza.
6 She ______________ probably tell you about it the next time she sees you.
7 Rocio and Peter ______________ come to the match on Sunday. They don't really like sports.

UNIT 5 — modals of request and permission: *could, can/can't, may*

Function

We use modals *could*, *can/can't*, and *may* to request and grant permission. We use *can* to ask for permission informally, whereas *may* and *could* are formal and more polite. We use *can't* to refuse permission, *can* to grant permission, and *may* to formally grant permission.

Form

Asking for permission	Granting permission	Refusing permission
Can I use your pencil?	Yes, you can.	You can't borrow my pencil.
Could we borrow your car?	Of course you can borrow my car!	You may not borrow my car.
May we go home now?	Yes, you may.	You may not.
Could I speak to you about that?	Yes, you can.	No, you can't.
May I have your phone number?	Yes, you may. It's …	No, you may not.

A Choose the correct option.

1 Can I / I can visit you next weekend?
2 No, you can't / can look at my homework.
3 May I / you ask your advice about something?
4 Yes, you may not / may.
5 May / Can we speak to you after class, Professor?
6 No, you can't / can.
7 "Could we sit here?" "Yes, you could / can."

B Unscramble and write the sentences.

1 I / open / can / window / the / ?

____

2 may / see / I / ID / your / ?

____

3 you / yes, / can / use / bike / my / .

____

4 yes, / may / you / now / go / .

____

5 can / address / have / your / I / email / ?

____

6 we / could / juice / more / orange / have / ?

____

UNIT 6 — present perfect with *for* and *since*

Function and form

We use the present perfect with *for* or *since* to talk about actions or situations that began in the past and continue in the present. *For* is used for a period of time, and *since* is used with a specific time. *How long* means *how much time*.

We form the present perfect with the auxiliary *have/has* and the past participle of the verb. With regular verbs, we form the past participle by adding *–ed*. Many verbs have irregular past participles.

Present perfect affirmative	Present perfect negative	Questions with *how long*
I've known her for five years.	I haven't known her for very long.	How long have I known you?
You've had this car for two months.	You haven't had that car for two months.	How long have you worked here?
She's lived here since 2016.	She hasn't lived here since 2016.	How long has it been like this?
He's studied here since January.	We haven't studied here since January.	How long has he felt like that?
We've been married for one year.	We haven't been married for one year.	How long have we driven for?
They've been there for a long time.	They haven't been there for a long time.	How long have they lived together?

A Read and choose the correct option.

1 I've known Maria for / since we were children.
2 She's been here for / since a long time.
3 They've driven to work together for / since years.
4 We've been members of that gym for / since last July.
5 She's had the same cell phone for / since two years.
6 I've worked with the same company for / since 2015.

B Complete the conversation using the prompts in parentheses.

Naomi: I want to do something different with my life. I am bored! **1** ________________ (I / live) in this area for a long time, and I need a change.
Aaron: Yes, you've been here **2** ________________ (a long time).
How **3** ________________ (long / you / have) this job?
Naomi: For about three years!
Aaron: Maybe you should take a vacation and take some time to plan your future. I saw some cheap flights to Greece yesterday. **4** ________________ (Have you / be / there)?
Naomi: No, I haven't! That's a good idea. **5** ________________ (I / not / have / vacation / since) last summer.
Aaron: **6** ________________ (It / be / long time / since) I've had a vacation, actually. I think I need to take a break, too!

UNIT 6 — present perfect with *ever* and *never*

Function

Ever and *never* refer to actions at an unspecific time in the past. *Ever* is used in questions and *never* is used with an affirmative verb.

Form

Questions with ever	Short answers	Never
Have you ever been to Greece? Have you ever ridden a motorcycle? Has she ever traveled the world?	Yes, I have. / No, I haven't. Yes, you have. / No, you haven't. Yes, she has. / No, she hasn't. Yes, we have. / No, we haven't. Yes, they have. / No, they haven't.	I've never been to Greece. I've never ridden a motorcycle. She's never traveled the world.

A Complete the conversation with the words from the box.

been ever have haven't never tried

Ben: I think I'd like to try the new restaurant that's just opened. Have you **1** ________ been there?
Sally: No, I **2** ________, but I've heard it's not very good.
Ben: Oh, really? What about the pizzeria on the main square? Have you ever **3** ________ it?
Sally: Yes, I **4** ________. I went there just last week. It's amazing; you should try it!
Ben: I think I will. My cousin's coming to visit this weekend. He's never **5** ________ here before, so I want to show him all the sights!
Sally: Is that your cousin from the US? I've **6** ________ met him before. You should introduce us!

B Match the halves to make sentences.

1 I've never eaten ____
2 Have you ever cooked ____
3 She's never been ____
4 They've never met before, ____
5 Have you ever swum ____
6 We've never traveled ____

a to my house, so I gave her directions.
b in the Atlantic Ocean?
c by plane, so we're a little nervous.
d but I think they'll like each other.
e Mexican food, but I want to try it.
f a meal for a big group of people?

UNIT 7 — present perfect with *already*, *just*, and *yet*

Function

We use *just* to show that an action has happened in the very recent past. We use *already* to show that an action has happened (sometimes sooner than expected). To show that an action is going to happen but hasn't happened, we use *yet* with the negative present perfect. To find out if an action has happened, we use the present perfect and *yet* in a question.

Form

already	*just*	*yet*
I've already started my new job. I've already applied for it.	I've just sent my resume. He's just called me. We've just met.	Have you met the boss yet? Have you thought about what you want to do yet? I haven't had an interview yet. They haven't contacted me yet.

A Unscramble and write the sentences for a conversation.

Luna: How's the job hunt going?
Henry: It's going well! **1** I've / PR firm / just / applied / for a job / with a
Luna: **2** seen / ! / I've / the perfect job / just / for you It's an internship at *Wave* magazine.
Henry: Oh! **3** that / already / I've / seen / job ad **4** I / sent / resume / haven't / my / yet
Luna: **5** interviews / yet / you / ? / had / have / any
Henry: **6** just / had / I've / an / email I have an interview with a news website on Friday.
Luna: That's great! Good luck.

1 ______________________________
2 ______________________________
3 ______________________________
4 ______________________________
5 ______________________________
6 ______________________________

B Choose the correct option.

1 She hasn't had any training **yet** / **already** because she's just started.
2 He's **already** / **yet** been promoted, and he's only worked there for a year!
3 I've **just** / **yet** gotten a raise! Let me buy the coffee this time.
4 Have you started working there **yet** / **just**?
5 They've **already** / **yet** gone home. They usually finish early on Fridays.
6 I've **just** / **yet** emailed her, so hopefully she'll reply soon.

UNIT 7 — present perfect and simple past

Function

We use the simple past to talk about an event that happened at a specific time in the past, to describe routines in the past, and to talk about events that happened at the same time or immediately after another event. We use present perfect to talk about an event that happened sooner than expected, to ask a question about whether something has happened, and to talk about an action that has been in progress for an amount of time, an action that happened in the very recent past, or an action that began in the past and will continue in the future.

Form

We form the simple past by adding *–ed* to the end of regular verbs. Some simple past forms are irregular. The present perfect is formed with the auxiliary *has/have* and the past participle.

	Present perfect	Simple past
Statements	I have (I've) lived here for five years. We have (we've) started a business together.	I lived here five years ago. We started a business together last year.
Questions and answers	Have you had breakfast? Yes, I have. / No, I haven't. Which countries have you visited? I've visited France and Egypt.	Did you have breakfast this morning? Yes, I did. / No, I didn't. Where did you visit last summer? I visited France.

A Read and choose the correct option.

Valerie: Hey, Zelia! I've just **1 had / have** a great idea. I'm going to start my own business.
Zelia: Wow! **2 Have you ever done / Did you ever do** anything like this before?
Valerie: No, **3 I worked / I've worked** at the same job since I graduated. I think it's time to do something different now.
Zelia: Cool! What are you going to do?
Valerie: Well, I've just **4 seen / saw** that there's a small building on Main Street for rent. I want to rent it and open my own restaurant.
Zelia: That's great! I've **5 thought / think** about starting a business, but I don't know if I could do it. You'll be great! Good luck.

B Complete the sentences with the present perfect or simple past form of the words in parentheses.

1 Hi, Sandra! ______________________________ (have) a good time last night?
2 Bob and I ______________________________ (work) at the same company for three years.
3 She ______________________________ (have) a job interview yesterday. I think it went well!
4 Last year, I ______________________________ (apply) for about 15 different jobs.
5 ______________________________ (see) my phone? I can't find it anywhere!

UNIT 8 — gerund phrases as subject and object

Function

A gerund is an *–ing* verb that functions as a noun. A gerund can be either the subject or the object of a sentence. We use a gerund after the verbs *prefer*, *enjoy*, *can't stand*, *like*, *love*, and *hate*.

Form

Gerund as subject	Gerund as object
Going outside on a cold and rainy day is fun. Spending time with you is always great! Painting is a really relaxing hobby.	Many people enjoy posting on social media. My friends love hanging out in the park. We always enjoy coming to visit you.

A Identify the errors and rewrite the sentences correctly.

Five Tips to Become More Creative

1 Face a blank page is always scary, but thinking up new ideas is great for your creativity.

____

____

2 If you hate brainstorm, why not try doing it with a friend? Two heads are better than one!

____

____

3 Do what you enjoy will help you feel more creative. Do you love be outdoors? Then get outside and enjoy some fresh air to help you think more clearly.

____

____

4 Be open to ideas is really important. If an idea doesn't work for you, then have another one.

____

____

5 Ask the right questions. Know what you want to do is probably the most important part of the creative process.

____

____

B Complete the sentences with a gerund phrase and a noun so that they are true for you.

1 __Doing__ (do) __yoga__ is a great way to help you relax and feel less stressed.
2 Lots of people enjoy ________ (go) ________ because they love nature.
3 ________ (join) ________ is a good way of meeting new people.
4 My family really likes ________ (spend) ________ together.
5 ________ (visit) ________ is a nice thing to do when you're in a new city.
6 My friends and I always enjoy ________ (have) ________ together.
7 My dad can't stand ________ (do) ________.

UNIT 8 — verb + gerund or infinitive

Function

Some verbs are followed by an infinitive (*to* + verb), while some verbs are followed by a gerund (verb + *–ing*). Some verbs (e.g., *like*) can be followed by either an infinitive or a gerund (this does not change the meaning).

Form

Love, like, hate, prefer **+ infinitive / *–ing* verb**	***Would like*** **+ infinitive**
I hate eating alone. We prefer to shop online. She likes eating out with friends.	He'd like to see her again. We'd like to stay a little longer. I'd like to thank you for your help.
Would prefer **+ infinitive**	***Would rather*** **+ base verb**
I'd prefer to travel by plane. She'd prefer to do it herself.	I'd rather see an action film. They'd rather know the truth.

A Read and choose the correct option.

Elena: Hey, it's the long weekend! Susie's rented a house at the beach, and she's invited us! Do you want to go?

Tom: Hmm, I don't know. Susie likes really action-packed vacations, and you know I prefer **1** chill out / to chill out.

Elena: I know you do! I like relaxing, too, but I hate **2** to waste / waste a holiday weekend doing nothing.

Tom: Well, we can compromise. Would you like **3** to go / going and spend the day with Susie?

Elena: Hmm, it's a long drive. I'd prefer **4** staying / to stay overnight. The house looks beautiful! Here's a picture.

Tom: Well, it does look nice. OK, let's go and stay overnight. I'd rather **5** stay / to stay Friday night than Saturday night, if that's OK. There's a football game on TV Saturday that I would really like **6** seeing / to see.

UNIT 9 — future forms: *will*, *going to*, present progressive, and simple present

Function

We use *will* or *going to* when we make predictions about the future. To talk about arrangements, we use present progressive, and to talk about intentions, we use *going to*. To talk about future events that are scheduled to happen, we use the simple present.

Form

will				
Affirmative			**Questions**	
I You He/She It We They	will/'ll	see you later. be back. do really well. all work out. eat here again. make friends easily.	Will you try harder next time? Will we go shopping?	
			Negative	
			She won't make that mistake again. It won't rain—the sky is blue.	

going to	**Present progressive**	**Simple present**
I'm going to study law. It's not going to rain. She's not going to live there. Are you going to travel?	You're having lunch. He's seeing her tomorrow. We're not getting up early. Is he visiting her tomorrow?	School starts at 9 a.m. We leave at 3 a.m. The train doesn't leave until tomorrow morning. When does the plane take off?

A Complete the conversations with words and phrases from the box.

are thinking   does   going to   I'm moving   we're meeting   we'll   won't   you'll

1 **Nicanor:** I'm tired of sharing an apartment. I'm ______________ start looking for a place of my own.
Luis: That's a good idea. Places are expensive, though. Do you think ______________ find something?

2 **Ellie:** We ______________ find an apartment in this neighborhood. Everything's so expensive!
Leah: Don't be so pessimistic! ______________ find something.

3 **Aria:** Have you heard the news? ______________ into a new apartment!
Pedro: Congratulations! When ______________ your lease start?

4 **Adara:** Mariam and I ______________ about sharing an apartment.
Batul: That sounds like a good idea!
Adara: ______________ later today to talk about it.

UNIT 9 — future possibility and certainty (*may*, *might*, *could*, *will*, *won't*, *probably*, *definitely*)

Function

We use *may*, *might*, and *could* to talk about things that are possible in the future. We use *probably* when we are almost sure about the future. We use *definitely* when we are very sure about the future.

Form

Future possibility	Future probability
I might go there. She may study there. They could move to a new house.	I'll probably come to the party.
Future certainty	**Negative future possibility**
I'll definitely email her.	He may not be happy. She might not like it.
Question form	**Short answers**
Do you think you might …? Do you think you'll …?	Yes, I might. / No, I might not. Yes, I definitely/probably will.

A Read and choose the correct option.

Cameron: What are your plans for next year? Do you think you **1 might / definitely** move out of your parents' house?

Janet: Yeah, I might. I'm not sure, though. I'm in my final year of college, so I'll **2 might / probably** have to study a lot more. I **3 probably / might** have to give up my part-time job, so I'll **4 probably / might not** have less money.

Cameron: Yeah, the final year is tough, believe me! You'll **5 may / definitely** have to study more. It **6 may / probably** be a good idea to stay with your parents for another year.

Janet: Why do you think that?

Cameron: Well, it's not always easy sharing an apartment. You **7 might / definitely** not get along with your roommates.

Janet: Yeah, I suppose you're right! Oh, well, Mom and Dad **8 probably / could** won't be upset if I hang around for another year.

B Unscramble and write the sentences.

1 an / rent / next / I'll / definitely / apartment / year / .

____

2 probably / share / we'll / bills / the / .

____

3 you / next / think / do / live / you'll / alone / year / ?

____

4 she / study / in / different / a / may / country / .

____

5 might / I / not / go / the / movies / to / .

____

6 our / apartment / balcony / have / new / won't / probably / a / .

____

7 definitely / they'll / be / tomorrow / there / .

____

UNIT 10 — zero and first conditional

Function

The zero conditional expresses general facts and scientific truths. The first conditional expresses real possibilities in the present or future. When the *if* clause is at the beginning of the sentence, it should be followed by a comma.

Form

Zero conditional	
***if* clause (*if* + present tense)**	**Result clause (present tense)**
If you eat well, If a person exercises every day,	you feel well. he or she feels more energetic.

First conditional	
***if* clause (*if* + present tense)**	**Result clause (will + base verb)**
If you drink more water, If she takes some time to relax,	your skin will look clearer. she'll feel better.

A Use the prompts in parentheses to complete the conversation.

Selena: I don't feel good. If I stand up quickly, **1** ______________________ (feel / dizzy).
Marco: You're working too hard. **2** ______________________ (work at computer) for hours without taking a break, you'll feel pretty terrible afterward.
Selena: You're right. I need to make some lifestyle changes.
Marco: Yeah, I think you do. You're working too hard, and you're not eating well. **3** ______________________ (make bad choices), you won't feel so good.
Selena: True! I don't have time to eat healthy meals.
Marco: It doesn't need to take a lot of time. If you drink more water, **4** ______________________ (stop / get headaches), for example. Drinking water doesn't take too much time, does it?
Selena: I guess not. And I suppose if I eat less sugar, **5** ______________________ (have / more energy)—isn't that what they say?
Marco: Yeah. **6** ______________________ (make / small changes), it's easier to keep going with them. Good luck!

UNIT 10 — second conditional

Function

We use the second conditional to talk about hypothetical or impossible situations in the present or future.

Form

***if* clause (*if* + past tense)**	**Result clause (*would, could, might* + base verb)**
If I lost my credit card, If I found a lost puppy, If she had a million dollars, If I was talented at music,	I would / I'd call the bank. I could take it home. she might start her own business. I'd learn to play the flute.
If I got lost in New York, If he told me his biggest secret,	I wouldn't panic. I wouldn't tell anyone.

A Read and choose the correct option.

What would I do if I **1** won / win a million dollars? Well, first of all, **2** I call / I'd call all my friends, and **3** I'll / I'd ask them to come to my house. Then **4** I'd / I'll have a big party. If I was rich, **5** I might want / I might wanting some new clothes, so my friends and I **6** would go / go shopping at our favorite stores. We'd **7** buy / bought some elegant clothes, and then we'd go to the best restaurant in town. **8** If / When we decided to eat at the best restaurant in town, we'd want to travel in style, so I think **9** I'd / I'll hire a limousine for the occasion.

B Identify the mistakes and rewrite the sentences correctly.

1 If you doing more exercise, you'd feel better.

____

2 If it snowed tomorrow, I go skiing.

____

3 If I lived near the beach, I learn to surf.

____

4 If they asked you to work for them, do you say yes?

____

5 What would you do if you'll miss the bus?

____

6 If you spoke a foreign language, you can get a really good job.

____

7 If we have a yard, we'd have a barbecue every night in the summer.

____

UNIT 11 — simple present passive

Function

We use the present passive to focus on the thing that receives the action, when we don't know who or what does something, when it's obvious or unimportant who or what does something.

Form

Affirmative		Negative	
Auxiliary *be* in simple present	**+ past participle of the verb**	**Auxiliary *be* in simple present + not**	**+ past participle of the verb**
Volkswagen cars are Indian films are Oranges are	made in Germany. shot in Bollywood. grown here.	Tiramisu isn't Grapes aren't	made from oranges. produced in Iceland.

A Complete the steps using the present passive.

How Glass Is Recycled

1 Glass / empty *The glass is emptied.*
2 Glass bottle / take / recycling center ______________________________
3 Glass / sort / by color ______________________________
4 Glass / crush and melt ______________________________
5 Glass / make / into new products ______________________________
6 New product / sell / stores ______________________________
7 Glass / empty / take / recycling center ______________________________

B Identify the mistakes and rewrite the sentences correctly.

1 Our room is be cleaned at the moment. ______________________________
2 English is speaked all over the world. ______________________________
3 Credit cards are accepting here. ______________________________
4 About 100,000 people are employ by this company. ______________________________
5 His invention is now sell in 45 different countries. ______________________________
6 Her name is knowing throughout the country. ______________________________

UNIT 11 — simple past passive

Function

We use the simple past passive to focus on the thing that received the action, when we don't know who or what did something, when it's obvious or unimportant who or what did something.

Form

Affirmative		Negative	
Auxiliary *was/were* in simple past	**+ past participle of the verb**	**Auxiliary *was/were* in simple past + not**	**+ past participle of the verb**
The biro pen was	invented by a Hungarian, Laszlo Biro.	I wasn't	invited to the party.
We were given	free coffee.	We weren't seen	by a doctor.

A Complete the text using the simple past passive forms of the verbs in parentheses.

I **1** ____________ (give) a really cool birthday present last Christmas—grass flip-flops! When you wear them, you feel like you're walking on grass. Grass flip-flops **2** ____________ (invent) by an Australian man who loved the feeling of grass under his feet!

My best-ever present **3** ____________ (give) to me by my best friend, Anna. It's a beautiful picture of a Scottish landscape, and it's special because it **4** ____________ (take) by her.

On my last birthday, I got a pair of socks. They **5** ____________ (knit) by my aunt, and they **6** ____________ (make of) hard, scratchy wool. I didn't like them very much!

UNIT 12 — reflexive pronouns

Function

We use reflexive pronouns when the subject and the object of the sentence are the same. We can also use reflexive pronouns to mean "without help from another person."

Form

Subject pronoun	Reflexive pronoun	Example
I	myself	I taught myself to dance.
You	yourself	Help yourself to food!
He	himself	He made himself a sandwich.
She	herself	She bought herself a coat.
It	itself	It switched itself off.
We	ourselves	We consider ourselves lucky.
You	yourselves	Did you build this yourselves?
They	themselves	They found themselves homeless.

A Match the halves to make sentences.

1 I was feeling cold, so I bought _____
2 It was a great feeling to find _____
3 You can teach _____
4 He doesn't see _____
5 Clara and Miguel found _____
6 Make yourself _____

a myself a hot drink.
b at home!
c themselves in a large, bright classroom.
d himself as an optimistic person.
e yourself just about anything nowadays.
f myself part of a big, friendly group.

B Complete the conversation with the words from the box.

do it myself herself motivate myself myself ourselves see myself yourself

Suki: I taught **1** ________________ to read Chinese when I was 10.

Malik: Wow—you taught **2** ________________? You must be really motivated.

Suki: Yeah, I suppose I do **3** ________________ as a motivated person.

Malik: That's impressive. I can never **4** ________________ to do things like that!

Suki: Well, I really wanted to go to China, and there were no language classes in my area, so I just had to **5** ________________.

Malik: That reminds me of my sister. She really wanted to learn ballet, but there were no classes in our area. She spent hours watching YouTube videos and she taught **6** ________________!

Suki: Wow! That's really cool! Hey, you're coming on the study trip to Germany next year, aren't you? Why don't we teach **7** ________________ German? Maybe you'd feel more motivated if we learned together.

Malik: Sure!

UNIT 12 — tense review

Function and form

Use	Example
We use the simple present to talk about a present state or habit. We also use the simple present to talk about a future scheduled event.	I share an apartment with some friends. The train leaves at three in the afternoon.
We use the present progressive to talk about an action in progress now. We also use the present progressive to talk about a future arrangement.	I'm waiting for my taxi to get here. We're meeting each other this afternoon.
We use the simple past to talk about a past state or habit.	I loved that TV show when I was younger!
We use the past progressive to talk about an action in progress at a past moment.	It was snowing when we were at the shops.
We use the present perfect to talk about a situation that started in the past and continues to the present moment.	She's been my teacher for three years now.
We use the second conditional to talk about hypothetical situations.	If I had a car, I'd give you a lift.

A Read and choose the correct option.

1 Have / **Did** you ever felt shy on your first day of a new job? When I started my new job, **2 I** / **I've** felt really nervous because I didn't know anyone. Then one day, when I **3 was leaving** / **left** the office, one of my colleagues asked me if I wanted to join the company's tennis club. I said, **4** "**I've** / **I** never played tennis before," but my colleague said it didn't matter. I decided to go along. Two years later, I **5 am knowing** / **know** a lot of people, and I don't feel shy anymore. In fact, next year **6 I'm playing** / **play** in a tennis tournament with some workers from another company! If I wasn't part of the tennis club, I think I **7 might not know** / **maybe don't know** so many people.

Macmillan Education
4 Crinan Street
London N1 9XW
A division of Macmillan Education Limited

Companies and representatives throughout the world

Speak Your Mind Level 2 Student's Book ISBN 978-1-380-03124-2
Speak Your Mind Level 2 Student's Book + access to Student's App and Digital Workbook ISBN 978-1-380-03118-1
Speak Your Mind Level 2 Student's Book + access to Student's App ISBN 978-1-380-03117-4

Written by Mickey Rogers, Joanne Taylore-Knowles and Steve Taylore-Knowles

The authors have asserted their right to be identified as the authors of this work in accordance with the Copyright, Designs and Patents Act 1988.

First published 2020

Designed by QBS Learning
Illustrated by Daniel Deamo (Lemonade) pp. 10, 50; Martina Farrow p. 21; Keith Favazza (Wendy Lynn & Co.) pp. 88, 102; QBS Learning pp. 60, 92, 109.
Original cover design by therestless.co.uk
Cover adaptation by Roberto Martinez
Cover photographs by **Getty Images**/Chatuporn Sornlampoo/EyeEm (background); **Shutterstock**/leungchopan (lower body), Shutterstock/Dima Sidelnikov (upper body), Shutterstock/ventdusud (window).
Picture research by Fernanda Rocha/Ikonia LLC

Authors' acknowledgements
Mickey, Jo and Steve would like to thank everyone at Macmillan Education and RedNova Learning who have made this project possible and who have gone the extra mile (literally!) to meet up, work together, and throw around a million ideas, some of which even made their way into the books! Jo and Steve would also like to thank Scout for her patience and understanding and for letting her parents get on with it when they needed to!

The publishers would like to thank all the teachers that piloted and reviewed the series, and a special thanks to Annette Flavel for content and cultural reviews.

The authors and publishers would like to thank the following for permission to reproduce their photographs:
Alamy Stock Photo/a-ts p. 22(7), Alamy Stock Photo/Andor Bujdoso pp. 86, 134, Alamy Stock Photo/Amy Cicconi p. 62(bl), Alamy Stock Photo/Hero Images Inc. p. 113, Alamy Stock Photo/Carolyn Jenkins p. 114(t), Alamy Stock Photo/Antony McAulay p. 24(tl), Alamy Stock Photo/parkerphotography p. 28(tr), Alamy Stock Photo/Jochen Tack p. 90, Alamy Stock Photo/Tetra Images, LLC pp. 92(3), 93, Alamy Stock Photo/Naho Yoshizawa/Aflo Co., Ltd p. 24(tc); **E+**/filadendron, TODOR TSVETKOV p. 12(br); **Getty Images** p. 62(3), Getty Images/ajr_images p. 83, Getty Images/Aliraza Khatri's Photography p. 34(tl), Getty Images/Markus Altmann p. 14(t), Getty Images/Luis Alvarez pp. 126, 138, Getty Images/Danilo Andjus p. 12(2), Getty Images/andresr pp. 26(br), 128, Getty Images/Yuri Arcurs p. 85, Getty Images/eli_asenova p. 12(6), Getty Images/Aurora Open/Steve Glass p. 102(br), Getty Images/Avalon_Studio p. 22(br), Getty Images/Katarzyna Bialasiewicz p. 130, Getty Images/Big Cheese Photo p. 12(1), Getty Images/BJI/Blue Jean Images p. 38(tl), Getty Images/Paul Bradbury p. 100(7), Getty Images/Adie Bush p. 77, Getty Images/Jasper Cole p. 78(4), Getty Images/dlerick p. 22(4), Getty Images/Dziggyfoto p. 78(2), Getty Images/EXTREME-PHOTOGRAPHER p. 61(mr), Getty Images/Geber86 p. 32(b), Getty Images/Hero Images pp. 38(tr), 40(tl, tr), 80(cl), Getty Images/iStockphoto/monkeybusinessimages p. 80(bl), Getty Images/Jamesmcq24 p. 22(5), Getty Images/Johner Images p. 94, Getty Images/Juanmonino p. 14(c), Getty Images/Jupiterimages p. 111, Getty Images/Maya Karkalicheva p. 64(t), Getty Images/Eva-Katalin p. 32(c), Getty Images/KatarzynaBialasiewicz pp. 46, 130, Getty Images/Ronnie Kaufman p. 40(m), Getty Images/Dennis McColeman p. 64(t), Getty Images/Mike Kemp p. 32(a), Getty Images/kuarmungadd p. 14(b), Getty Images/Loop Images/Craig Joiner p. 62(4), Getty Images/LWA p. 12(3), Getty Images/Emilija Manevska p. 12(8), Getty Images/Maskot p. 62(6), Getty Images/Meridian Studios p. 42(a), Getty Images/Mikeh57 p. 19, Getty Images/Milkos p. 38(tmr), Getty Images/Josef Mohyla p. 18(tr), Getty Images/Tara Moore p. 44, Getty Images/Thomas Northcut p. 110(tr), Getty Images/NoSystem images p. 84, Getty Images/ollo p. 34(cr), Getty Images/HUGO PHILPOTT/Staff p. 114(b), Getty Images/Alex Segre/Contributor p. 64(cr), Getty Images/Ariel Skelley p. 24(tr), Getty Images/Smith Collection/Gado/Contributor p. 34(b), Getty Images/Serghei Starus/EyeEm p. 92(5), Getty Images/Tinpixels p. 48(cr), Getty Images/Omar Vega/Contributor p. 8, Getty Images/Westend61 pp. 48(tr), 80(tl), Getty Images/Todd Wright p. 42(b); **Hero Images** pp. 66, 132; **Purestock**/Punchstock/Getty Imagesty Images p. 61(bl); **Science Photo Library**/TEK IMAGE pp. 106, 136; **Shutterstock**/aerogondo2 p. 12(4), Shutterstock/Africa Studio pp. 92(4), 105(tl), Shutterstock/ajt p. 115, Shutterstock/aklionka p. 124, Shutterstock/amasterphotographer p. 58(tc), Shutterstock/AnastasiaKopa p. 100(3), Shutterstock/ArtFamily p. 82(br), Shutterstock/ArtOfPhotos p. 77, Shutterstock/A StockStudio p. 52(br), Shutterstock/belushi p. 50, Shutterstock/Claudia K p. 42(c), Shutterstock/design56 p. 22(1), Shutterstock/ESB Professional p. 125(1), Shutterstock/Evgeny Atamanenko p. 92(7), Shutterstock/beeboys p. 91, Shutterstock/Beer5020 p. 67, Shutterstock/bellena p. 110(bl), Shutterstock/Dmitry Bruskov p. 62(7), Shutterstock/Vasiliy Budarin p. 27, Shutterstock/Diego Cervo p. 100(8), Shutterstock/chainarong06 p. 105(tm), Shutterstock/CHAjAMP p. 100(6), Shutterstock/Tasha Cherkasova p. 74(t), Shutterstock/Chinnapong p. 97, Shutterstock/dnd_project pp. 96, 135, Shutterstock/DNF Style p. 12(7), Shutterstock/Orest Drozda p. 52(tr), Shutterstock/Vikentiy Elizarov p. 107, Shutterstock/ESB Professional p. 72, Shutterstock/flower travelin' man p. 38(br), Shuttestock/Anna Gorodnitskaya p. 122(1), Shutterstock/gpointstudio p. 125(3), Shutterstock/Kaspars Grinvalds pp. 12(5), 36, 129, Shutterstock/g-stockstudio p. 122(2), Shutterstock/Images By Kenny p. 22(6), Shutterstock/JM Travel Photography p. 70, Shutterstock/Just dance pp. 56, 131, Shutterstock/Kamira p. 110(tm), Shutterstock/kazim95 p. 58(br), Shutterstock/Kingcraft p. 110(br), Shutterstock/Olesya Kuznetsova p. 78(3), Shutterstock/Teerasak Ladnongkhun p. 22(2), Shutterstock/lassedesignen p. 7, Shutterstock/Soloviova Liudmyla p. 117, Shutterstock/LukaKikina p. 110(bm), Shutterstock/Mariyana M p. 22(8), Shutterstock/Muskoka Stock Photos p. 120(br), Shutterstock/Nattakorn_Maneerat p. 100(2), Shutterstock/Maridav p. 100(4), Shutterstock/Natalia Mels p. 104, Shutterstock/MinDof p. 18(tl), Shutterstock/Monkey Business Images p. 99, Shutterstock/Monster Ztudio pp. 116, 137, Shutterstock/tanya_morozz pp. 104-105(b), Shutterstock/Luciano Mortula - LGM p. 62(2), Shutterstock/Mr.anaked p. 112(b), Shutterstock/MyImages - Micha p. 92(2), Shutterstock/NATNN p. 109, Shutterstock/Ollyy pp. 76, 133, Shuttestock/OPOLJA p. 120, Shutterstock/P A p. 122(3), Shutterstock/pathdoc p. 37, Shutterstock/Pavel L Photo and Video p. 30, Shuttestock/Sean Pavone p. 62(br), Shutterstock/panotthorn phuhual p. 110(tl), Shutterstock/Igor Plotnikov p. 87, Shutterstock/Valeri Potapova p. 62(1), Shutterstock/Dmitrii Pridannikov p. 92(1), Shutterstock/pryzmat p. 62(8), Shutterstock/raksapon p. 110(br), Shutterstock/Rawpixel.com pp. 40(b), 54, 118, 141, Shutterstock/rozbyshaka p. 17, Shutterstock/Huguette Roe p. 112(t), Shutterstock/SAPhotog p. 28(cl), Shuttestock/S.Borisov p. 62(5), Shutterstock/Panwasin seemala p. 28(cr), Shutterstock/ShotPrime Studio p. 108, Shutterstock/sirtravelalot p. 100(1), Shutterstock/Ljupco Smokovski p. 28(br), Shutterstock/Oleksii Stebliuk p. 123, Shutterstock/StockLite p. 105(tr), Shutterstock/pathdoc p. 15, Shutterstock/Roman Samborskyi p. 38(tml), Shutterstock/Joseph Sohm p. 64(br), Shutterstock/Constantin Stanciu p. 16, Shutterstock/Mila Supinskaya Glashchenko p. 82(tr), Shutterstock/Syda Productions p. 125(2), Shutterstock/Romolo Tavani p. 57, Shutterstock/Binh Thanh Bui p. 22(3), Shutterstock/VasiliyBudarin p. 27, Shutterstock/Viktoriya p. 98, Shutterstock/vipman p. 92(6), Shutterstock/viputae p. 47, Shutterstock/Tom Wang p. 68, Shutterstock/wavebreakmedia p. 125(4), Shutterstock/WAYHOME studio pp. 32(d), 42(d, tr), Shutterstock/Trudy Wilkerson p. 55, Shutterstock/yurakrasil p. 78(1), Shutterstock/88studio p. 74(bl); **123RF**/Monchai Tudsamalee p. 100(5).

Additional sources:
p. 36 – Nigel Lindemann, "What's the average survey response rate? [2018 benchmark]," *Survey Anyplace*, 2018. p. 66 – "How to Become an Architect: Education and Career Roadmap," Study.com website. p. 76 – Adobe, *State of Create Study*, 2012; IBM, *CEO Study*, 2010; Scott Barry Kaufman, 2014 (cited by John Paul Titlow, "7 Surprising Facts About Creativity, According to Science," *Fast Company*, 2016). p. 82 – Oliver Burkeman, "Five Reasons Why We Should All Learn How to Do Nothing," *The Guardian*, 2015. p. 98 – Bryan Roche, "10 Ways to Improve Your Brain Health," *Psychology Today*, 2014; Hannah Nichols, "How to Boost Your Brain," *Medical News Today*, 2018; Joseph Mercola, "Nine Ways to Make Yourself Smarter," Mercola.com, 2012; Michael Grothaus, "This Is the Only Type of Brain Training that Works, According to Science," *Fast Company*, 2017. p. 108 – mcc_northcutt, "55 Things You Probably Didn't Know About T-Shirts," *The BlueCotton Blog*, 2016. p. 126 – "Entrepreneurship Rankings," U.S. News & World Report, 2018.

Printed and bound in Brazil

2025
55